Literacy and Social Responsibility

Literacy and Social Responsibility

Multiple Perspectives

Edited by
Frances Christie and
Alyson Simpson

Published by Equinox Publishing Ltd.

UK: 1 Chelsea Manor Studios, Flood Street, London SW3 5SR

USA: DBBC, 28 Main Street, Oakville, CT 06779

www.equinoxpub.com

First published 2010

© Frances Christie, Alyson Simpson and contributors 2010

British Library Cataloguing-in-Publication Data

A catalogue record for this book is available from the British Library.

ISBN   978 1 84553 642 8   (hardback)
ISBN   978 1 84553 643 5   (paperback)

Library of Congress Cataloging-in-Publication Data

Literacy and social responsibility : multiple perspectives / edited by
Frances Christie and Alyson Simpson.
  p. cm.
  Includes bibliographical references and index.
  ISBN 978-1-84553-642-8 -- ISBN 978-1-84553-643-5 (pbk.) 1. Language
and languages--Study and teaching. 2. Literacy--Study and teaching. 3.
Sociolinguistics. I. Christie, Frances. II. Simpson, Alyson.
  LB1576.L55254 2010
  302.2'244--dc22
  2010012401

Index prepared by Fiona Sim
Typeset by Steve Barganski
Printed and bound in Great Britain by Lightning Source UK Ltd, Milton Keynes

Contents

1 Literacy and social responsibility   1
Frances Christie and Alyson Simpson

2 Literacy as a theme in educational theory and in policy   9
Frances Christie

3 Multiple literacies: implications for changed pedagogy   24
Alyson Simpson and Maureen Walsh

4 Socially responsible literacy education:
toward an 'organic relation' to our place and time   40
Peter Freebody

5 Literacy and the Arts   56
Robyn Ewing

6 The social context of literacy acquisition:
achieving good beginnings   71
Tony Vinson

7 The experience of Youth Off The Streets   87
Father Chris Riley and Karelynne Randall

8 Beating educational inequality with an integrated
reading pedagogy   101
David Rose

9 Enhancing literacy education for refugee children   116
Denise Lynch

vi   *Contents*

10 Envoi   130
   Frances Christie and Alyson Simpson

Index   137

1   Literacy and social responsibility

Frances Christie and Alyson Simpson[1]

Introduction

Few educational issues stir public debate and discussion more often and more volubly than literacy. Community interest in it seems high, given the range of newspaper articles that regularly report aspects of literacy: student literacy performance in school, literacy levels in the workforce, programmes to promote improved literacy teaching, and/or periodic laments about literacy standards. Moreover, governments throughout the English-speaking world devote significant financial resources to literacy education, while teacher education programmes, typically of some years' duration, attach importance to the preparation of teachers to teach literacy. And, so the evidence suggests, with some frequency, governments call either for new inquiries into the teaching of literacy or for new policy and curriculum statements to do with the teaching of English, in which literacy has always an important role. Thus, for example, in England, following the deliberations of various committees and working parties, the first statement of English in the National Curriculum appeared in 1995, and it has been periodically updated since (see Qualifications and Curriculum Authority 2009), while other initiatives have addressed specific areas of literacy teaching (e.g., The Rose Report 2006, devoted to teaching early reading). In the USA, much attention was given in the 2000s to the federal government programme known as No Child Left Behind (NCLB), in which billions of dollars were spent to reshape classroom literacy practices. The results, though initially judged rather variable in quality, led to the Reading First Final Report (Gamse *et al.* 2008), while the work of No Child Left Behind continues, revised in the light of ongoing experience (see Commission on No Child Left Behind 2009). Like the Rose Report on reading and the subsequent Rose Report on the Primary Curriculum (Rose 2009), No Child Left Behind recommended that literacy programmes should focus on higher order learning skills, as well as back-to-basics literacy principles.

In Australia, following various federally funded initiatives in language and literacy policy (see Christie 2003 for a longer discussion), the first White Paper on *Australia's Language: The Australian Language and Literacy Policy* appeared in 1991. After a change of government, this was followed by a policy statement, *Literacy for All: The Challenge for Australian Schools* (1998), and in 2005 by the National Inquiry into Literacy (see Christie in chapter 2). At the time of writing this chapter, Australia was preparing a new National English Curriculum, to be released in 2010, in which the teaching of literacy was to be a prominent theme. In all, in the early twenty-first century, literacy is very much on the national agenda of all English-speaking countries, though there is often disagreement about definitions of literacy, about methods for its teaching and assessment, and about the overall significance of literacy in the contemporary world.

One of the many issues over which there has been disagreement, at least in the recent past, has been the significance to be accorded literacy in national development. Graff (1987: 1-11) for example, questioned what he said had been some widely held assumptions about the relationship of literacy and social and economic development, both in North America and Western Europe, such that the spread of literacy was held to contribute to the growth of a nation. The empirical evidence to support this view was not strong, he argued, while the nature of literacy was itself more problematic than the view acknowledged. Literacy was more diverse than conventional views often recognised, and its functions in social and cultural processes were very complex, for literacy, like oral language, had attitudinal, ideological and ideational values, none of which might be easily measured in testing regimes. Freire and Macedo (1987: 141-59), writing rather differently, proposed a radical critique of literacy and its significance, arguing that any literacy should be viewed 'as a set of practices that functions to either empower or disempower people'. Writing mainly of the experience of people in postcolonial countries, including Africa, they argued that literacy taught in the national language of the colonising country (e.g., Portugal) had an oppressive function, serving only to continue the domination of the people, not least because it perpetuated the values of the oppressing nation. Literacy in this situation could only be 'emancipatory and critical' (Freire and Macedo 1987: 159) when 'conducted in the language of the people', so that the socially and culturally significant meanings expressed in that language were preserved. Learners might, it was acknowledged, later progress to literacy in the colonialist language. Relatedly, Freire and Macedo argued, following Giroux (1983), much English literacy teaching in English-speaking countries such as the USA, based as it often was on impoverished models of 'back-to-basics' reading programmes, also served to oppress people, offering them only the 'utilitarian' literacy skills necessary for a docile workforce. A richer model of literacy would acknowledge its power in constructing meaning and its values in building personally rewarding and critical understandings in learners.

There is a sense in which we can agree with aspects of such critiques. It does not necessarily follow, for example, that the spread of literacy causes significant national development, for the interplay of movements in history is often more complex than that might suggest. However, such movements are often in some way related. The *World Bank Report for 2009: Reshaping Economic Geography* notes that 'today's generation by almost any global summary measure of income welfare is better off than any previous generation in human history' (The World Bank 2008: 110). While there is still 'considerable income divergence between the richest and poorest countries', levels of education are said to have improved, and literacy levels over the last two centuries are shown to have steadily increased throughout the world (The World Bank 2008: 110). No easy causal connection between levels of education and of literacy and economic advance is assumed in the World Bank discussion, though it is difficult to escape the conclusion that they are at least correlated. For example, the OECD in noting the results of several International Adult Literacy Surveys conducted in 1994, 1996 and 1998 (see Kirsch 2001) observes that 'literacy affects, *inter alia*, labour quality and flexibility, employment, training opportunities, income from work and wider participation in civic society' (OECD 2009). The surveys showed that those with the lowest levels of literacy were typically more likely to be unemployed than those with higher literacy levels. Literacy does matter, and it does make a difference, both in the history and development of nations, and in the lives of their many citizens.

As for the critique to do with literacy and oppression in modern countries, one can agree that some methods for teaching literacy – those loosely associated with various 'back-to-basics' approaches – are limited and insufficient in introducing learners to productive and rewarding ways of using literacy. In that sense, they might be said to 'oppress'. However, this is a matter of poor pedagogy, and there are available many more enlightened and richer approaches to the teaching of literacy, some of which are discussed in this volume.

We can also agree with the general observation associated with both sets of critiques that literacy, like oral language, is a sociocultural phenomenon, centrally involved in the negotiation and construction of meanings of many kinds. Literacy is not a neutral phenomenon, and in modern English-speaking countries possession of literacy is a very important aspect of personal identity, conferring access to many ways of making meaning, forms of knowledge, information and entertainment; it necessarily also confers capacity to create such meanings for oneself. This is as much an issue for second-language users of a language as for mother-tongue speakers. Thus, for those children and adults who come to a new English-speaking country with languages other than English, it is certainly important to respect their literate codes, acknowledging that they represent valued ways of making meaning having sociocultural significance. Nonetheless, they also need opportunity to master the ways of making meaning of English literacy, for this is to facilitate acceptance and entry to the society they have adopted, and in which they need to feel they belong (see Lynch, chapter 9). Overall, literacy is a resource which, once mastered, brings significant benefits to all who possess it, while those who lack adequate literacy levels often feel marginalised, their life choices seriously circumscribed.

Why literacy and social responsibility?

This book brings together a number of scholars from language and literacy education and from social work, all of them interested in literacy. The dialogue this sets up is less common than one might think, for social workers and literacy educators, while no doubt well disposed to each other, do not often unite in the writing of a book on literacy. Yet each potentially has much to offer the other. The different approaches to research methodology and the varied collections of data on which the chapters are based give an insight into the terrain of education and social work, providing a number of different perspectives on literacy and our responsibilities towards those in need of literacy education. In this sense the perspectives offered are 'multiple' as the title of the book suggests. Yet there is another sense in which the discussions offered are 'multiple', because literacy itself is understood in 'multiple' terms. More than one contributor to the volume asserts that literacy has many dimensions, for while the term embraces funda-mental preoccupations with reading and writing the written code, it also embraces the literacies of the modern world of Information and Communication Technologies (ICT) (see Simpson and Walsh, chapter 3). Moreover, there are many senses in which literacy can be considered: in terms of its role in learning, in promoting personal development, in fostering self-expression and self-esteem, and in conferring skills that build employability. These are among the several themes addressed by the writers in this book.

Overall, the writers in this volume would argue the importance – and indeed the social responsibility – of a just society in teaching literacy to all.

Some important themes

One of the many themes that emerge in the discussions developed in this book is the importance of early intervention in the teaching of literacy to the very young. Vinson, for example, writing out of a lifetime in social work, argues the critical value of early intervention in helping very young children in difficult socio-economic circumstances prepare for, and adjust to, the demands of schooling. Such demands include such things as: engaging in constructive talk conducive to learning, participating with others in shared learning tasks, entering with under-standing and interest into the nature of print, and taking pleasure in the enchantment of books. While all such activities are available to many young children as an aspect of their preschool experience, for many others they are very unfamiliar, as Rose points out, in discussing the needs of young Australian Aboriginal children living in poorly resourced communities. All young children, including the advantaged, benefit from rich learning activities that, among other things, reveal the values of literacy as a means of gaining entry to knowledge and ideas, though those born to social disadvantage need particular support and assistance to overcome such disadvantage. Vinson in particular, aware of the many sad pathways by which the disadvantaged make their way to prisons as adult offenders, is clear that early intervention in educational provision, which includes early literacy teaching, is essential in breaking the cycles of social dislocation and dysfunction found in many communities.

Social disadvantage is also addressed by Father Chris Riley and his colleague Karelynne Randall, who are both involved in a successful Sydney-based programme, Youth Off The Streets, dedicated to saving disaffected youth, many of whom are adrift 'on the streets', and beyond the capacity of their families to nurture and protect. Successful programmes for adolescents such as these embrace far more than their needs in literacy, for the youth are often damaged by various forms of abuse and neglect. However, successful mastery of literacy is also seen as a critical aspect of the total package of support and advice given the young in helping them turn around years of alienation and achieve a positive sense of well-being and self-worth. For these individuals, literacy offers a pathway towards employment opportunities. However, as programmes like the EDEN project demonstrate, there is a flow-on effect as the young people are encouraged to recognise the value of sharing their learning with others who need support.

Developing a positive sense of self-worth is a theme also addressed by Lynch, discussing the needs of refugee children and youth, many of whom struggle to make their way in the modern world. Drawing mainly on Australian experience, Lynch discusses various groups: children who travel from their country of origin with parents or guardians, those who travel unaccompanied (often the most vulnerable), those who are not strictly children though also not old enough to function independently. Some are held in detention with their parents, though in Australia at least mandatory detention for children has been abandoned. Overwhelmingly, all the evidence regarding these children and youths points to their need for a sense of safety and positive well-being; developing literate skills in the language of their host country is one essential aspect of their achieving such safety and security, for it assists them in adjusting to schooling and to the wider community they have joined.

Issues of literacy and positive well-being are important for many of the writers here, apart from those most directly involved in the problems of social work. Ewing, for example, writing of the arts and literacy, argues for the values of a model of literacy which recognises the contribution of the arts to teaching and learning about literacy: artistic expression, whether in writing and reading or in related activities of drama and music, enriches the learner and helps build a strong sense of identity. Literacy in this sense is for imaginative experience, for enlightenment and for pleasure, as well as for access to the skills needed for learning in other ways in the curriculum.

A broad set of concerns with literacy for learning is featured by all writers, including those like Christie, who reviews a little of the history of the word 'literacy', arguing that until very recent times the term was taken to refer primarily to reading, rather than to reading and writing: to that extent, she suggests, the nature of writing has often been not well acknowledged, its significance not sufficiently foregrounded for the purposes of teaching and learning. The nature of the written language, it can be shown, is different from speech, and it takes some years to master the written code. Moreover, written language changes as children mature and move from the primary to the secondary years, increasingly learning the particular kinds of literacy associated with different subject disciplines of a secondary education. This is a matter also discussed by Freebody, who in addition discusses the importance of teacher-led talk in building a shared understanding of the language of school disciplines. The teaching of literacy is intimately bound up with the learning of knowledge. Literacy and the knowledge it expresses in the twenty-first century will be if anything more complex, more unpredictable and more varied than in even the recent past. Hence, what will matter in learning literacy will be the acquisition of portable skills in handling and manipulating the written code in all its manifestations, the better to deal with the challenges of life in a challenging world.

In a complementary sense, Rose writes in particular of the importance of teaching reading to facilitate entry to the disciplinary knowledge of school learning, and hence for entry to the wider life of further study or employment. He outlines the pedagogical principles he and his colleagues have evolved over years of working with many disadvantaged children and young adults, teaching skills in reading texts, while also scaffolding effective writing. The text-based approach he provides is rigorous both in its attention to the nature of the written language to be mastered and in its concern for the specialist areas of knowledge that will increasingly preoccupy learners as they grow older and mature.

Simpson and Walsh, while also interested in the language of school knowledge, discuss the nature of literacy in a multiliterate, multimodal context. Their brief review of current terminology sketches some of the complexity of an area where definitions of what counts as literacy are contested. The classrooms of the twenty-first century, they argue, will increasingly draw both on the 'traditional' skills of reading and writing print materials, and on the visual and/or digital texts, in which the interplay of visual and verbal is already creating new kinds of literacy.

In examining the various modes of communication necessary for students to function successfully in the classrooms of today, questions are raised about current pedagogy. The answers to these questions have implications for future policy if it is to account for multiple forms of literacy.

Conclusion

Interwoven across all the themes taken up is a sense of urgency about English literacy and its teaching and learning, for it contributes to the overall development of persons, enriching their lives in many senses. Possession of good literacy skills is essential as a necessary part of a rewarding education, just as it can contribute to a generally rewarding life. It can confer access to information, knowledge and ideas of many kinds, while it can also open up imaginative areas of experience in literature and the arts more generally. The English-speaking nations of the twenty-first century do indeed have a broad social responsibility to ensure literacy programmes of a high order. This volume aims to contribute to discussions of literacy and its teaching, identifying some of the sources of literacy difficulties, while also suggesting possible pedagogies for addressing these.

References

Australia's Language: The Australian Language and Literacy Policy (1991) Canberra: Australian Government Publishing Service.

Christie, F. (2003) English in Australia. *RELC Journal: A Journal of Language Teaching and Research in South East Asia* 34 (1): 100-19.

Freire, P. and Macedo, D. (1987) *Literacy: Reading the Word and the World.* London: Routledge and Keegan Paul.

Gamse, B., Tepper Jacob, R., Horst, M., Boulay, B., Unlu, F., Bozzi, L. *et al.* (2008) *Reading First Impact Study: Final Study* (No. NCEE 2009-4038). Washington, DC: National Centre for Education Evaluation and Regional Assistance: Institute of Education Sciences.

Giroux, H. (1983) *Theory and Resistance: A Pedagogy for the Opposition.* South Hadley, MA: Bergin and Harvey.

Graff, H.J. (1987) *The Labyrinths of Literacy. Reflections on Literacy Past and Present.* Lewes and Philadelphia: The Falmer Press.

Kirsch, I. (2001) *International Adult Reading Survey (IALS): Understanding what was Measured.* Research Report RR-01-25, December 2001. Educational Testing Service. Statistics and Research Division Princeton NJ 08541

Literacy for All: The Challenge for Australian Schools (1998), Canberra: Commonwealth Department of Employment Education and Training.

National Inquiry into Literacy, The (2005) http://www.dest.gov.au/nitl/report.htm (accessed 17 May 2009).

No Child Left Behind (2009) Commission on No Child Left Behind, Aspen Institute http://www.aspeninstitute.org/policy-work/no-child-left-behind/about-commission

/secretary-tommy-g-thompson-governor-roy-e (accessed 25 August 2009).

OECD (2009) Literacy in the information age: final report of the international adult literacy survey. http://www.oecd.org/LongAbstract/0,3425,en_2649_39263294_39437981_1_1_1_1,00.html (accessed 25 August 2009).

Qualifications and Curriculum Authority (2009) *The National English Curriculum*. http://curriculum.qcda.gov.uk/key-stages-3-and-4/subjects/english/index.aspx (accessed August 2009).

Rose Report, The (2006) *Final Report of the Independent Review of the Teaching of Early Reading*. London: Department for Education and Skills. http://www.standards.dcsf.gov.uk/phonics/report.pdf (accessed 9 May 2009).

Rose, J. (2009) *Independent Review of the Primary Curriculum: Final Report* (No. DCSF-00499-2009). Nottingham: Department for Children, Schools and Families.

World Bank, The (2008) *World Bank Report for 2009: Reshaping Economic Geography*. Washington, DC: The International Bank for Reconstruction and Development/World Bank.

Notes

[1] **Frances Christie** is Honorary Professor of Education and of Linguistics at the University of Sydney and Emeritus Professor of Language and Literacy at the University of Melbourne. She has worked for many years in language and literacy education and has had a considerable research and publishing record in the area. Recent books have included: *Classroom Discourse Analysis: A Functional Perspective* (London and New York: Continuum, 2002); *Language Education in the Primary Years* (Sydney: University of NSW Press, 2005); with J.R. Martin (eds.), *Language, Knowledge and Pedagogy: Functional Linguistic and Sociological Perspectives* (London and New York: Continuum, 2007); with B. Derewianka, *School Discourse: Learning to Write across the Years of Schooling* (London and New York: Continuum, 2008).

Alyson Simpson is a senior lecturer at the Faculty of Education and Social Work at the University of Sydney. She teaches in undergraduate and postgraduate pre-service teacher programmes and supervises research candidates studying in the area of literacy/English education. Her research projects have examined designs for e-learning and concepts of visual literacy in higher education and primary schools. She is the co-author of *Children's Literature and Computer Based Teaching* (London: Oxford University Press, 2005) and author of *Reading under the Covers: Helping Children to Choose Books* (Newtown: Primary English Teaching Association, 2008).

2 Literacy as a theme in educational theory and policy

Frances Christie[1]

Introduction

State-sponsored compulsory education is less than two centuries old, and notions of curriculum, of childhood and of pedagogy have changed in many ways. At the end of the nineteenth century reading and writing skills were not understood in any unitary or singular sense, so that the two were taught as discrete skills. The term 'literacy' was not in use, even in the early twentieth century, and the word came into use only in the latter part of that century. As the twenty-first century dawned, a great deal had changed. Literacy had become a major theme in government policy in all English-speaking nations, while significant resources were devoted to the professional preparation of teachers to teach literacy. Adoption of the term 'literacy', rather than reading and writing, represents a significant gain, underscoring the fact that they are two aspects of the same phenomenon: namely, using written language. However, despite the apparent advance in educational theory and practice with the adoption of the term 'literacy', there remain some enduring problems in literacy education, themselves a legacy of its history and of a time-honoured tendency to create false dichotomies or 'dualisms' where none really exist. Other such dichotomies found in English language and literacy education, for example, have included those between 'process' and 'product' or 'form' and 'function' in writing. In all such cases the distinction has some heuristic value, in that it can throw light on different aspects of some process or activity. However, the claim that the two can be genuinely separated is both misleading in terms of educational theory and unhelpful in terms of pedagogical practice. I shall argue in this chapter that the problems arise because of a lack of an adequate theory of language. Such a theory will, among other things, provide an explanation of the grammatical differences between speech and writing, seeing them as manifestations of the same linguistic system, which children learn to deploy for a range of purposes as they mature, and a model for tracing the developmental changes in control of literacy that occur with the movement from childhood to adolescence.

The origins of the dichotomies referred to were old. However, they achieved a particular prominence in the drive to promote and extend opportunity to large numbers of children in the elementary schools of the nineteenth century. In such schools the educational goals were in many ways quite limited, and their aspirations for the teaching of reading and writing reasonably constrained. Much has changed since the appearance of widespread elementary or primary schooling, and the levels of educational attainment required in the twenty-first century are greater than in the past. High levels of literacy performance are needed in the contemporary world as an essential aspect of the educational attainments sought. Moreover, a great deal of current educational research suggests the wisdom of adopting a model of literacy studies that is based on an adequate theory of language, stressing the interrelated nature of reading and writing, and the manner in which the written language changes as children grow and move from the primary into the secondary school years. It is in the transition from childhood to adolescence (when children also pass from the primary to the secondary school) that written language changes quite markedly, as I shall argue, and it is no accident that it is then that many children begin to drop behind in their school performance.

The role of reading and writing in early elementary schooling

From their inception, the first state-sponsored schools attached importance to the teaching of reading in particular, though writing, arithmetic, numeracy and a little 'general knowledge' were also involved. Reading was particularly valued for the ability it gave to read religious and other 'improving' texts, while the extension of the franchise as the century proceeded was also used to justify the teaching of reading: anyone who could vote should be able to read, it was argued. The focus of state-sponsored education as it emerged in the nineteenth century in Britain, its colonies and in America was on the elementary school, and while forms of secondary education were available, it was around matters to do with the purpose, provision and maintenance of elementary schools that most official activity developed. In Britain, the churches commenced their involvement through the nineteenth-century Sunday schools, and later through various schools using monitorial systems (e.g., Bell 1823; Lancaster 1803), by which large numbers of pupils were drilled by monitors working under the supervision of a master. It was only reluctantly that it was accepted that the state should be involved in taking responsibility for elementary education. This was principally because in the large cities, such as London, Manchester or Glasgow, numbers of children had appeared who were unschooled, unlettered and indeed ungoverned (Hunter 1994). Something needed to be done, it was argued, in the interests of bringing such children into some degree of order and enlightenment. In the Australian colonies, similar problems were recognised quite early. In New South Wales (NSW), for example, soon after the first white settlement was established in 1788, colonial governors realised that some schooling needed to be provided for the children of free settlers, convicts and emancipists, and they began to take some measures to deal with the problems.

Those who took an early reforming interest in such matters, in both Britain and America, tended to look for a model to the experience of Prussia, where the *Volksschule* had appeared in the eighteenth century, designed for the education of the peasantry. In America, where the first schools that had emerged by the eighteenth century had been private, the early reformer Horace Mann (see Cremin 1957) in Massachusetts was instrumental, in 1837, in setting up a system of 'common schools', based to some extent on the Prussian example, and offering an education that was non-sectarian and free; the model was taken up in other parts of the country as the century proceeded. In Britain, educational reformers such as David Stow in Scotland (1854) or James Kay-Shuttleworth in England (1973) developed models for the education of the urban poor. In the Australian colony of NSW, state-funded bodies were providing elementary schooling by the middle of the nineteenth century; by the end of it, the principle had been won that education should be 'free, compulsory and secular' (The Public Instruction Act, 1880), though the compulsory provision was not effective until after the First World War.

Evidence for the dominating role of reading in the elementary curriculum is apparent from the curricular guidelines, inspectorial reports and teacher training manuals (e.g., Gill 1883; Robinson 1867; Dunn 1837), in all of which reading rated considerable attention. Writing was also deemed important and timetabled for, though the word 'writing' referred not as it tends to do today, to the act of composing in written language, but to the task of mastering the writing system. Thus, for example, in NSW, children normally started to learn to shape their letters on slate, or sometimes paper, relatively soon after commencing school, but they did not undertake any sustained writing in the sense of writing 'compositions' (which might be no more than a sentence or two) until they had completed three or four years of schooling. And since most children did not stay at school beyond the third year (if they stayed that long), most did not learn to compose sustained written language (Christie 1976).

Apart from information from educational sources, evidence of the impact of the distinction between reading and writing may be found in the shipping lists kept by the NSW Immigration Board in the nineteenth century. Ships carrying assisted immigrants plied between Britain and the Australian colonies, and passengers were required to indicate whether they could read *or* write (New South Wales State Archives nd). While most passengers said they could do both, a sizeable minority of adults regularly indicated they could read, but not write.

Without the capacity to write, creating written texts of their own, individuals who could claim ability to read alone had at best a very limited literate capacity.

One of the many manuals of the nineteenth century written for the benefit of teachers in training (Fitch 1880) cited the authority of Locke:

> When a boy can read English well, it will be seasonable to enter him into Writing. Not only children, but any body else that would do anything well should never be put upon too much of it at once, or be set to perfect themselves in two parts of an action at the same time, if they can possibly be separated ... (Locke, 1693, *On Working Schools*, cited in Fitch 1880: 223).

Such a claim appealed to educational reformers looking to establish schools for large numbers of children in which pedagogical steps might be adopted, reducing the learning to a process of measured stages. The logic might seem reasonable, though it denied the advantages children would enjoy were they encouraged to move freely between reading and writing. In the history of the human species, after all, writing systems were invented first, and reading necessarily emerged as an accompanying activity. As the twentieth century was to show, pedagogical methods which foreground the connectedness of the two practices, affirming the importance of both in creating and interpreting meaning in written language, are most successful in developing literate capacity. By the 1960s, for example, with the Breakthrough to Literacy Programme (see Mackay, Schaub and Thompson 1989), developed out of work with teachers as part of the Nuffield/Schools Council Programme in Linguistics and English Teaching, directed by Halliday (see discussions in Hasan and Martin 1989; Christie and Unsworth 2005), the principle was established that young students should engage with reading and writing even in their earliest years of schooling. The very name of that programme – Breakthrough to Literacy – was significant, marking a break with past educational theory and practice.

The advent of 'literacy'

The word 'literate' dates from the fifteenth century, according to the Oxford English Dictionary. A literate person was one of letters, though this normally meant one who could read. The noun 'literacy', somewhat surprisingly, is relatively recent, dating from the late nineteenth century, and according to the Oxford English Dictionary, it first appeared in an educational journal in the USA in 1883. Despite its appearance by the early twentieth century, the word was not in extensive use in educational documentation until the latter part of that century. In the aftermath of the Second World War, UNESCO organised regional meetings concerned to address the problems of 'illiteracy' in many parts of the world (Tanguiane 1990: 9), and these led in time to the International Literacy Year in 1990. In the English-speaking world, among educational specialists and administrators as well as English teachers, the words 'reading' and 'writing' were most commonly used for much of the century, while the use of 'language' only became a feature of curriculum statements after the 1970s, reflecting the impact of extensive research into language and its role in learning that emerged in the UK, the USA and Australia from the 1960s on (see discussions in Christie and Rothery 1979, and Green, Hodgens and Luke 1997). With the emergence of talk of 'language development' or 'language education', attention turned increasingly to 'literacy', initially as an aspect of language education, though towards the end of the twentieth century and into the twenty-first literacy and its development achieved a significance of its own, while new terms such as 'multiliteracies', 'visual literacy', 'musical literacy', 'computer literacy' or 'critical literacy' had appeared. Indeed, so generally is the word 'literacy' now used in many contexts that there is a risk that its meaning will be lost. I refer here to expressions like 'financial literacy' or even 'emotional literacy', which I have encountered in the daily press. Of course, such uses are metaphorical, though one wonders how useful they really are.

Overall, and whatever the merits of many metaphorical uses, where once the term 'literacy' was rarely, if ever, used in much educational policy or pedagogical theory, it has now become quite common, even commonplace, and large numbers of publications devoted to it – books and journals – regularly appear, while significant amounts of government funds are devoted to literacy programmes in schools. Moreover, all governments in the modern world – not only those in the English-speaking countries that are the focus of this chapter – are committed to provision of literacy education. In many ways, such a development is desirable because, as I suggested above, use of the word 'literacy' rather than 'reading and writing' serves to emphasise the intimate relationship of the two phenomena involved in using written language.

Literacy is often equated with reading

However, literacy is still often equated with reading in many parts of the world. Consider, for example, the case of Australia's most recent National Inquiry into Literacy (2005), the title of whose report actually read *Teaching Reading* – in my view a curious name in itself, given the apparent commitment to literacy. The Executive Summary for this report read in part, 'Underlying this report is the conviction that effective literacy teaching, and of reading in particular, should be grounded in findings from rigorous evidence-based research'. A little later the statement went on to refer to the teaching of reading as 'a key element of literacy' (National Inquiry into Literacy 2005 Executive Summary: 11). No-one would question the claims for the importance of reading, though what constitutes 'evidence-based research' has been the subject of disagreement since the report appeared. More serious, however, is the absence of mention of writing in the Executive Summary. The whole report reveals a marked preoccupation with reading, and while some acknowledgement is made of the need to teach writing, it does not receive detailed discussion, while such 'evidence-based research' as is referred to in the literature review includes none devoted to writing. A particular attention is given to 'systematic, direct and explicit phonics instruction'. One recommendation states that 'literacy teaching (should) continue throughout schooling (K–12) [kindergarten to year 12]' (National Inquiry into Literacy, 2005 Executive Summary: 12). Such a recommendation is commendable, though the absence of discussion of what constitutes writing development – or indeed, reading development – and how it changes across the years K–12, is unfortunate.

The preoccupation with reading at the expense of writing, at least in the English-speaking world, is often bound up with heated arguments that surface periodically over phonics and the teaching of reading (see, for example, Snow and Juel 2005; Christie 2006). Teaching phonics is important, but this can often be allowed to obscure the fact that achieving control of phonics is, for most children, a learning task for the early years (though older students may need assistance where their early teaching has not been effective, and students of English as a second language, like those discussed in chapter 9, also need assistance). Moreover, in order to be effective, the teaching of phonics must itself be embedded in programmes devoted to reading for meaning, where this involves learning to control not only the spelling and writing systems, but also the organisation of the written sentence, and of the larger written text. To engage with the latter matters is to start to learn about the grammar of written language, though such learning extends well beyond the early years. The English acknowledged the importance of early years phonics when they called for the recent *Final Report of the Independent Review of the Teaching of Early Reading* (Rose Report 2006; no relation to Rose, an author in this book!) whose focus, as the name suggests, was on early years reading; in that case, early writing also received some attention.

Another source of recent information regarding the preoccupation with reading may be found in the Programme for International Student Assessment (PISA) studies, conducted by the OECD, and devoted to assessing performance among 15-year-olds in reading, mathematics and 'scientific literacy'. The surveys are conducted periodically, the last occurring in 2006, involving 57 countries and several languages. The tests measure reading ability and 'problem solving' and their aim is to assess 'how far students near the end of compulsory education have acquired some of the knowledge and skills that are essential for full participation in society' (OECD 2007: 1). Incidentally, Kress (2002: 11) has noted the limitations of the preoccupation of PISA with reading competence.

Reading ability is an essential, but insufficient, measure of literacy capacity, and writing ability is as much a measure of ability to participate in society as is reading ability. Indeed, there are grounds for arguing that a student's ability to write is very revealing of overall literate capacity. That is because writing is the productive rather than the receptive mode, and where students can achieve a degree of reading proficiency, they do not always achieve the same proficiency when they need to write themselves. In fact, by age 15, when students sit the PISA test, the kinds of written language students need to produce are of a quite demanding nature, and very different in character, meaning and linguistic organisation from the texts required in the primary years. Where students fail to grasp the nature of the written language they need to produce by adolescence, they do indeed start to fall behind. Furthermore, since in the contemporary world adolescents are normally expected to complete a secondary education, it is essential that we establish better understandings than hitherto of the literacy demands of the secondary years, where this must involve engaging with their writing. The rather minimal standards of literacy of the nineteenth and early twentieth centuries will no longer serve.

Problems in adolescent control of literacy have begun to be recognised, though the extent to which they are identified with writing performance varies. In the USA, for example, the difficulties of students entering the secondary school are sometimes spoken of in terms of the 'literacy gap' (e.g., Strickland and Alvermann 2004; Snow and Biancarosa 2003). While the problems are still often discussed as primarily to do with reading, there are signs of change. The Carnegie Corporation, for example, is currently promoting a major project for Advancing Literacy (Carnegie Corporation of New York 2008, initiated in 2003), arguing that up to about the third grade of school, reading programmes have proved reasonably successful, but that 'the knowledge base for how to teach reading for grades beyond this point is very thin'. The Corporation website goes on to note:

> The educational community faces a difficult challenge, since what is expected in academic achievement for middle and high school students has significantly increased, yet the way in which students are taught to read, comprehend and write about subject matter has not kept pace with the demands of schooling (Carnegie Corporation of New York 2008: 1).

This is a significant admission about the teaching of reading, while the recognition that students need help with their writing as well is very welcome. Other evidence is emerging that writing is receiving increased attention, for example in the work of the National Commission on Writing (2003), whose report referred to writing as the 'Neglected "R"'. Snow and Biancarosa (2003) and Biancarosa and Snow (2004) have also addressed writing performance in the USA. In Australia we have seen a series of government-funded initiatives since the late 1970s devoted to literacy performance in what was once called the 'interface' between primary and secondary schooling (e.g., Maling-Keepes and Keepes 1979), and later in the 'middle years', while in England, the National

Literacy Strategy (Department for Education and Skills and Qualifications and Curriculum Authority 2006) is currently devoted to improving general literacy performance in the junior secondary years, when children are aged 11 to 14 years.

All such initiatives are useful. They will be most effective, however, where they are informed by an understanding of the manner in which the literate language changes by late childhood to adolescence. The changes involve moves towards increasing abstraction, a necessary feature of the language needed to handle generalisation, discussion, argument, explanation and detailed description, all found in the writing of the secondary-school subjects as well as much writing of adult life. Where the written language of the early years is in many ways close to speech – since that is what the young know best – the written language of the secondary school becomes more remote from speech, its character often very dense. While the changes certainly have consequences for what children must read, they are in many ways best understood by looking at what children must write.

The changing nature of literate language by adolescence

Children pass through a series of developmental phases in their writing, from childhood, to late childhood and early adolescence, then to mid- and late adolescence, and thence to adult life. Some children of course pass more quickly through these phases than others, and they are not to be understood in any lock step manner. Many children do not ever achieve adequate control of the literacy of adolescence. Overall, when children commence writing, they deal with simple experience, moving on, by late childhood to adolescence, to some developing capacity to elaborate upon, and extend the experience about which they write; the language hence becomes denser, the meanings more abstract as various changes in capacity to organise ideas are facilitated. Children are able to compress more information in their writing than before, building increasingly abstract information. By mid- to late adolescence, successful students can express very abstract meanings indeed, as they handle interpretation, generalisation, value judgement, argument and symbolic meanings of various kinds. Some examples will illustrate the points made, though a more comprehensive discussion is found in Christie and Derewianka 2008. Most examples, apart from the first, will be taken from subject English, though I shall use some from other subjects, for the changes are not specific to any one subject.

Consider the following by a girl of five, with its simple series of clauses containing minimal information expressed in its nominal groups (or noun phrases) and its verbal groups:

I go shopping

Then we go home.

Dad comes home.

Granny comes home.

Then Grandad comes.

Then they go away.

The little girl is aware that she is writing about a series of events, for the clauses are connected, partly by the repetition of references to herself or to her family members, and partly by use of the temporal conjunction *then*. A slightly later development occurs when a six-year-old child writes thus:

We saw a stuffed dog,

It looked nice and fluffy,

where the writer shows a growing capacity to link clauses. Later on, children become more skilled in control of what is put first in their clauses, building coherence across more than one clause, as in this, by a boy aged 11:

Last summer holidays my family and I went to South West Rocks

I was really excited because we always have so much fun there.

In South West Rocks the surf isn't too rough.

By late childhood, successful students are able to expand their nominal group structures (or noun phrases), helping to compress a great deal of information, while also creating a series of interconnected clauses, as in this, by a boy aged nine years (where // denotes a clause boundary, and nominal groups are noted):

The king stepped off his carriage // and **the very moment [[he did]]** the crowd gasped // as they saw // **their great ruler and beloved king** stride onto **the wooden platform** // to **announce the two duelists [[who would serve the offering]]**.

(Note that the squared brackets [[ ]] indicate an embedded clause. A clause is deemed embedded when it fits within the nominal group, expanding on the meaning of the noun within that group.)

Again by late childhood, among other things, students learn to vary the disposition of their clauses, and the way information is made prominent for their readers. The following example is from a story by a boy aged 11, where << >> displays a dependent clause, which has been 'repositioned' in order to foreground its meaning:

> It was really hot on the rocks // so << when we finished lunch >> Nic turned to Mum // and said…

The unmarked way to write this would have been:

> It was really hot, so Nic turned to Mum when we had finished, and said …

Another example, from an older writer, aged 14, occurs in a story:

> As time went by more and more people entered and << with security guards standing on every corner of the building >>, no one could think // that anything would happen with the tight security like this.

Now consider the following by a girl of 12, whose clauses are relatively few, but who is able to compress quite a lot of information about her subject:

> William Shakespeare was an English poet and playwright, widely regarded as the greatest writer in the English Language and the world's pre-eminent dramatist.

Note the way in which information is compressed in the elliptical clause[2] whose nominal groups are quite large – *widely regarded as **the greatest writer in the English Language** and **the world's pre-eminent dramatist**.*

This capacity to expand the fundamental resources of language is critical, allowing the following student – a boy of 14 – to build a sense of atmosphere and excitement as his story unfolds (large nominal groups are indicated, and double slashes indicate clause boundaries):

> With **the awakening of the sun's rays, thousands of curious people** were on their way // to see **the spectacular display of jewellery in the enormous newly-opened museum.**

Here the compression of information is considerable, for if we expressed this in the more congruent manner of speech, it would be:

> When the sun rose in the morning // thousands of curious people were on their way // to see the spectacular display of jewellery in the museum // which had been newly opened.

Where the written version has only two clauses, the latter version has four, and this is significant because the tendency of written language is to reduce the number of clauses in sentences, compressing information in various ways.

As the vocabulary used by successful students expands, the capacity to build value judgement and interpretation also matures, as in the following from a film review, written by a boy aged 14, as part of the English programme:

> 'Who Framed Roger Rabbit' is a movie about a man's struggle [[to face his fears]], and a Rabbit's struggle [[to clear himself of murder]].

Here the writer uses two large nominal groups, containing embedded clauses, to create abstract phenomena, about which the text will unfold: *a man's struggle [[to face his fears]]; a Rabbit's struggle [[to clear himself of murder]]*. Clever students of English learn to offer such pronouncements, offering generalisations about the texts they read or view; they enable writers to create value judgements with regard to the text, allowing them to go on and make selective use of detail and event in order to support what has been declared. Weak students tend not to master such facility, often getting lost in detail about plot or character, without being able to offer interpretation of the meanings of texts read, or films viewed.

One finds the same capacity to build generalisation and interpretation in history, as well as value judgement, as in the following by a boy aged 16:

> The 25th of April, Anzac (Australian and New Zealand Army Corps) Day, is one of Australia's most important national occasions. It marks the anniversary of the first major military action [[fought by Australian and New Zealand forces during the First World War]].

Note again the large nominal groups here: *one of Australia's most important national occasions; the anniversary of the first major military action [[fought by Australian and New Zealand forces during the First World War]]*, each of which creates an abstraction, and around these the discussion will be developed. Such language is well away from speech.

As a general principle, the written language of adolescence and of adult life tends to be removed from the immediate actions of life, creating more abstract formulations of experience, whether these be about human relationships as in literature, human actions and their consequences as in history, or the phenomena observed in science, where the following is by a boy aged 17:

> Non-destructive testing is a method of analysing a material in such a way [[that the material is still safe for further use]]…Different types of non-destructive testing include visual inspection, dye penetrant test, magnetic particle testing, acoustic monitoring, x-ray testing and ultrasonic testing.

The latter text extract makes considerable use of technical language particular to the knowledge being expressed, and it is in fact a very dense text. Yet the density is a feature of the written language of all subjects by the mid- to latter years of adolescence. It is found for example in the following by a 17-year-old girl discussing a class novel:

> Mark Haddon's novel 'The Curious Incident Of The Dog In The Night-time' demonstrates that people's perceptions of the world are often hindered by a lack of understanding and empathy. Christopher's individual perception of his ideal world was uniquely displayed in the novel. The novel explored many relationships of deception between characters as well as false illusions. These relationships demonstrated the physical, psychological and emotional aspects of the characters' worlds including perceptions and understandings between characters.

This is a dense piece of writing, in which the writer draws back from the novel to offer judgements and interpretation of it and its values. Note how much the text depends on the abstractions built in its nominal groups: *people's perceptions of the world*; *a lack of understanding and empathy*. Note too, the metaphorical expression involved in several verb choices: *the novel **demonstrates** that people's perceptions...*; *the novel **explored** many relationships...*; *these relationships **demonstrated**...*

This is writing of a very abstract order, well away from the immediacy of speech. There is considerable skill involved in mastering the written language in such a manner, deploying its resources to achieve the 'design' that Myhill (2009) has argued is the mark of the successful student of written language.

The long journey in controlling the grammar of writing commences in childhood, and while much needs to be achieved by late childhood, this is also the point at which, when entering adolescence, children need to move into emergent control of a written language that compresses information in some senses, while its also expands and elaborates upon information in other senses.

Conclusion

The introduction of state-sponsored education in the nineteenth century marked an important step in the evolution of modern states and in the range of responsibilities the state assumed towards its peoples. From the start, it was deemed important to teach the young to read and write, though in practice reading received more attention from policy makers, educational theorists and teachers alike. Reading and writing were in any case conceived as discrete skills, and a strong view prevailed for a long time that reading should be taught first before children commenced their writing. The distinction made between reading and writing, both in terms of educational theory and in terms of pedagogy, was unfortunate, for it rested on an unsatisfactory model of language, denying the intimate relationship of the two modes of using written language. In the twentieth century, gains were made in language education, apparent, among other matters, in the steady assumption of the use of 'literacy', rather than reading and writing. Yet the relationship of reading and writing, in the English-speaking world at least, has remained uneasy, while the claims of writing development are often not well understood. As I have argued in this chapter, there is a significant series of changes in control of written language that must occur if children are to pass successfully from childhood to adolescence, evident in the grammatical organisation of the various texts they must write. While it is true that the changes are also apparent in the texts they must read, it will be particularly in the productive mode of writing that students will reveal how well they have mastered the nature of the written mode. In the twenty-first-century world, in which all students need to achieve a high level of literacy performance, schools have a responsibility to ensure much more than the reasonably minimal levels of literacy that applied in an earlier age.

References

Bell, A. (1823) *Mutual Tuition and Moral Discipline; or Manual of Instructions for Conducting Schools through the Agency of the Scholars Themselves*, 7th edn. London: G. Roake.

Biancarosa, G. and Snow, C.E. (2004) *Reading Next: A Vision for Action and Research in Middle and High School Literacy: A Report from Carnegie Corporation of New York*. Washington, DC: Alliance for Excellent Education.

Carnegie Corporation of New York (2008) *Advancing Literacy*. http://www.carnegie.org/literacy/index.html (accessed 8 May 2009).

Christie, F. (1976) The teaching of English in elementary schools in New South Wales 1848–1900: an inquiry into social conditions and pedagogical theories determining the teaching of English'. Unpublished MEd thesis, University of Sydney.

Christie, F. (2006) Literacy teaching and current debates over reading. In R. Whittaker, M. O'Donnell and A. McCabe (eds.) *Language and Literacy: Functional Approaches*. London and New York: Continuum, 45-65.

Christie, F. and Derewianka, B. (2008) *School Discourse: Learning to Write across the Years of Schooling*. Continuum Discourse Series. London and New York: Continuum.

Christie, F. and Rothery, J. (1979) English in Australia: an interpretation of role in the curriculum. In Maling-Keepes and Keepes 1979: 197-242.

Christie, F. and Unsworth, L. (2005) Developing dimensions of an educational linguistics. In R. Hasan, C. Matthiessen and J.J. Webster (eds.) *Continuing Discourse on Language: A Functional Perspective*, I. London and Oakville: Equinox, 217-50.

Cremin, L.A. (ed.) (1957) *The Republic of the School: Horace Mann on the Education of Free Men*. New York: Teachers College Press.

Department for Education and Skills and Qualifications and Curriculum Authority (2006) *A Condensed Key Stage 3: Designing a Flexible Curriculum*. http://www.standards.dfes.gov.uk/secondary/keystage3/all/respub/ks3flexcurricupd025906 (accessed 17 May 2009).

Dunn, H. (1837) *Popular Education, or the Normal School Manual: Containing Practical Suggestions for Daily and Sunday School Teachers*. London: Sunday School Union.

Fitch, J. (1880) *Lectures on Teaching*. Cambridge: Cambridge University Press.

Gill, J. (1883) *Introductory Text Book to School Education, Method and School Management: A Treatise on the Principles, Aims and Instruments of Primary Education*, new edn. London: Longmans, Green.

Green, B., Hodgens, J. and Luke, A. (1997) Debating literacy in Australia: history lessons and popular f(r)ictions. *The Australian Journal of Language and Literacy* 20 (1): 7-24.

Hasan, R. and Martin, J.R. (eds.) (1989) *Language Development: Learning Language, Learning Culture. Meaning and Choice in Language. Studies for Michael Halliday*. Norwood, NJ: Ablex.

Hunter, I. (1994) *Rethinking the School: Subjectivity, Bureaucracy, Criticism*. Sydney: Allen and Unwin.

Kay-Shuttleworth, J. (1973) *Four Periods of Public Education as Reviewed in 1832, 1839, 1846, 1862*, with an introduction by N. Morris. Brighton: Harvester Press.

Kress, G. (2002) English for an era of instability: aesthetics, ethics, creativity and design. *English in Australia* 134: 15-23.

Lancaster, J. (1803) *Improvements in Education as it Respects the Industrious Classes of the Community, Containing a Short Account of its Present State, Hints towards its Improvement, and a Detail of Some Practical Experiments Conducted to that End*, 2nd edn. London: Darton and Harvey.

Mackay, D., Schaub, P. and Thompson, B. (1989) The 'breakthrough' connection: 'breaking through the sound barrier into the written word', In Hasan and Martin 1989: 333-48.

Maling-Keepes, J. and Keepes, B.D. (eds.) (1979) *Language in Education: The Language Development Project Phase 1*. Canberra: Curriculum Development Centre.

Myhill, D. (2008) Towards a linguistic model of sentence development in writing. *Language and Education* 22 (5): 271-88.

Myhill, D. (2009) 'Becoming a designer: trajectories of linguistic development'. In R. Beard, R. Myhill, D.A. Riley and J. Riley (eds.) *The Sage International Handbook of Writing Development*. London: Sage, 402-14.

National Commission on Writing (2003) The neglected 'R' http://www.nwp.org /cs/public/print/resource/2432#neglected (accessed 17 May 2009).

National Inquiry into Literacy, The (2005) http://www.dest.gov.au/nitl/report.htm (accessed 17 May 2009).

New South Wales State Archives (nd) Assisted immigrants arriving in Sydney and Newcastle, 1844–59. Records held in New South Wales State Archives, Sydney.

OECD (2007) *Programme for International Student Assessment* http://www.oecd.org /document/22/0,3343,en_2649_34487_39713238_1_1_1_1,00.html (accessed 7 May 2009).

Robinson, R. (1867) *Teacher's Manual of Method and Organization adapted to the Primary Schools of Great Britain, Ireland and the Colonies*, 2nd edn. London: Longmans Green.

Rose Report, The (2006) *Final Report of the Independent Review of the Teaching of Early Reading*. London: Department for Education and Skills. http://www.standards.dcsf .gov.uk/phonics/report.pdf (accessed 9 May 2009).

Snow, C.E. and Biancarosa, G. (eds.) (2003) *Adolescent Literacy and the Achievement Gap: What Do we Know and Where Do we Go from Here? Carnegie Corporation of New York Adolescent Literacy Funders Meeting Report*. New York: Carnegie Corporation of New York.

Snow, C. and Juel, C. (2005) Teaching children to read: what do we know about how to do it? In M. Snowling (ed.) *The Science of Reading: A Handbook. Part VII Teaching Reading*. London and New York: Blackwell, 5-24.

Stow, D. (1854) *The Training System: Moral Training School and Normal Seminary for preparing School Trainers and Governesses*, 10th edn. London: Longman, Brown and Longmans.

Strickland, D.S. and Alvermann, D.E. (eds.) (2004), *Bridging the Literacy Achievement Gap, Grades 4-12*. New York and London: Teachers College Press.

Tanguiane, S. (1990) *Literacy and Illiteracy in the World: Situation, Trends and Prospects. International Year Book of Education*, XLII. Paris: UNESCO.

[1]   **Frances Christie** is Honorary Professor of Education and of Linguistics at the University of Sydney and Emeritus Professor of Language and Literacy at the University of Melbourne. She has worked for many years in language and literacy education and has had a considerable research and publishing record in the area. Recent books have included: *Classroom Discourse Analysis: A Functional Perspective* (London and New York: Continuum, 2002); *Language Education in the Primary Years* (Sydney: University of NSW Press, 2005); with J.R. Martin (eds.), *Language, Knowledge and Pedagogy: Functional Linguistic and Sociological Perspectives* (London and New York: Continuum, 2007); with B. Derewianka, *School Discourse: Learning to Write across the Years of Schooling* (London and New York: Continuum, 2008).

[2]   An elliptical clause is one in which some words have been left out: the full clause here would read, 'who is widely regarded as the greatest writer in the English Language and as the world's pre-eminent dramatist'

3   Multiple literacies: implications for changed pedagogy

Alyson Simpson and Maureen Walsh[1]

Introduction

This chapter is written at a time when heads of government use mobile technologies to reach the public via instant messages and when school children deal comfortably with multiple simultaneous modes of communication (more often at home than at school). Developments in digital and mobile technology have contributed to radical changes in communication, and these developments have significant implications for the definition of literacy in the twenty-first century and for its applications within educational contexts. As new technologies enable classrooms to be connected, not only via corridors, but also by networks of electronic pathways, this chapter aims to show how the social context of school and concepts of literacy have been significantly altered.

As a result of the changes that new technologies have had on communication, the nature of literacy itself has changed. Old concepts of literacy must be newly defined. In this fast-developing context, familiar ways of making meaning remain, but they are embedded, enveloped and sometimes made strange when combined with unfamiliar technologies. Take, for example, the teenager who reads hits on her Facebook page through her iPhone or the young child who uploads and organises family photos into a photo story. Each of these scenarios involves a range of learning opportunities that have the potential to be transferred into the classroom. The challenge to educationalists, within this new environment, is to devise pedagogy that will support literacy development successfully. Can the principles from old pedagogies stay relevant when literacy is enacted in such different ways in the twenty-first century?

In the recent decade, governments in the US, UK and Australia have acknowledged the need for revolutionary educational change that is futures oriented, supporting equity for all. It is clear that, while significant funding has been given to improving access to technology, current educational policy continues to be bound largely by traditional concepts of print-based literacy. Fortunately, in very recent times it appears as if some of the most restrictive policies will be rejected in favour of more open, richer pedagogy as a result of research that has shown that limiting the teaching of literate practices to 'the basics' is neither successful nor socially equitable. The findings of the UK Rose Report released in April 2009 (Rose 2009) and the USA *Reading First Impact Study: Final Study* released in December 2008 (Gamse *et al.* 2008) point towards the need for integrated approaches to literacy that resist reductionist, back-to-basics principles. Australia is in a unique period of reform as this chapter is being written. The creation of a National Curriculum presents an opportunity for Australian policy to be informed by principles of equity and diversity as well as being futures oriented to 'prepar[e] students for their lives in and beyond school' (National Curriculum Board 2009: 6).

Where chapter 2 discussed the emergence in the twentieth century of the word 'literacy' in educational theory and practice, stressing the interrelated nature of reading and writing, this chapter seeks to describe the literacy of the twenty-first century, exploring its range of practices. In doing this, the authors aim to provide a theoretical context within which new classroom practices can be framed. This theoretical context has introduced terms such as '21st century literacies' (National Council of Teachers of English 2007) , 'new literacies' (Coiro, Knobel, Lankshear and Leu 2008; Lankshear and Knobel 2003), 'multimodality' (Kress 2003; Kress and van Leeuwen 2001), or 'multiliteracies' with its various interpretations (Cope and Kalantzis 2000; Healy 2008; Unsworth 2001) and even 'digital literacy' (Merchant, 2009) into the lexicon. After a discussion of this theoretical context, we present evidence from research studies to show examples of what schools and universities are doing to ensure that not only will students have control of minimal levels of literacy but they will also have rich opportunities to build multiple literacies appropriate to their current and future lives.

Theories of literacies within new communication environments

Educational theorists have attempted to capture and define new communication environments. As one term emerges that seems to capture the changes in literacy practices, a further change occurs. We focus on this changing landscape by examining the terms 'new literacies', 'multimodality' and 'multiliteracies' below. Each bears some relation to each other, and each depicts aspects of the impact of changed literacy practices within social contexts. These different yet interrelated perspectives demonstrate attempts by educational researchers to establish a basis for new pedagogy, and these are now described in turn.

New literacies

The relationship between using print, media and information technology has been described as creating *new* literacies for some time (Gee 1996; Lankshear and Knobel 2003). Literacy has always been guided by developments in technology but Coiro *et al.* (2008), in their discussion of the way new literacies have emerged with the growth of the Internet and ICTs, specifically consider the 'evolutionary history' (Coiro, Knobel, Lankshear and Leu 2008: 2) of the relationship between literacy and technology since the 1960s and social change. They show literacy as being about the ability to adapt continually to new technologies and emphasise the impact of the Internet on social practices of literacy. Usage of the term 'new literacies' is commonly associated with ICTs and 'ways of knowing in a digital age' (Yelland *et al.* 2009: 5) and also incorporates 'new textual practices' (Comber and Kamler 2005: 119).

Multimodality

The theory of multimodality, particularly developed through the work of Kress and van Leeuwen (2001), has contributed to understandings about how various modes of print, language, image, movement, graphics, animation, sound, music and gesture create meaning. These modes are different semiotic or meaning-making resources, and meaning may be created through one or more modes, separately or simultaneously. Multimodal practices may include the combination of different modes in texts as well as the interaction between people, and between people and texts. As Kress and van Leeuwen have shown, 'meaning is made in many different ways, in the many different modes and media which are co-present in a communicational ensemble' (Kress and van Leeuwen 2001: 111). By studying classrooms as multimodal learning environments, several researchers (e.g., Bearne *et al.* 2007) have demonstrated the learning potential within modes other than language or the reading and writing of print-based texts (Kress *et al.* 2001).

Multiliteracies

While multimodality is concerned with the relationship between modes and the processing of modes, the term 'multiliteracies' refers more to the actual practices of literacy, implying that many different literacy practices are needed for communicating in contemporary society. Evolving from the theorising of the New London Group (Cope and Kalantzis 2000), the term 'multiliteracies' was concerned with the many types of communication needed in new and different social and cultural contexts, and for both print and electronic texts. The concept of multiliteracies informed a specific pedagogy framed by Cope and Kalantzis and adopted by many educationalists in the US and particularly South Africa. It has moved into a further pedagogical framework entitled Learning by Design (Healy 2008; Kalantzis and Cope 2005) which highlights the design element needed for producing texts in digital environments. The concepts and applications of multi-literacies have been expanded in a different way through the work of Unsworth (2001) who focuses on multidimensional, multiple literacies, particularly curriculum literacies needed within classrooms. Unsworth's work on discipline-based literacies makes explicit the need for teachers to perceive the relevance of literacy across all subject areas, particularly image–text relationships, and the way meanings can be constructed across modes.

Implications

The development of these related theories demonstrates that the concept of literacy can no longer be confined to the reading and writing of print-based texts. Each of the terms attempts to explain new processes of literacy within multiple media and modes of communication. Moreover, such terms represent attempts to define a 'textual landscape' (Carrington 2005) that itself is constantly changing. In 1997 the question was asked, 'what kind of literacies are important in a context of change?' (Lankshear et al. 1997: 2). It appears we are still answering that question as the context continues to change. Perhaps, as Sefton Green suggests, educationalists need a 'tactical' definition of literacy to prompt policy makers to plan ahead for future-focused transformative practices (Sefton Green in Livingstone 2008: 37). To meet the goal of improving educational outcomes for all students we must ensure that teachers are not 'preparing learners for tomorrow's needs by teaching yesterday's skills' (Lankshear and Knobel 2003: 105). The next section of the chapter presents two case studies from recent research into contrasting educational contexts to assess how the literacy practices within education programmes can support the needs of students living in a new millennium.

Research into educational contexts

While theorists are debating the significance of changes in literacy practices and attempting to define them, educators are faced with the practical challenges of adapting to these changes. Whether in school or tertiary contexts, teachers are required to plan learning experiences that incorporate new information and communication technologies. There are varied ways in which teachers across the sectors are responding to these challenges, and these responses will differ according to the types of resources available along with the willingness of teachers to engage with new pedagogy. Two examples located in educational settings, one situated in a primary school and the other in an urban university, are now discussed and analysed. The two case studies, completed by the authors Walsh (2008) and Simpson (Simpson and Preston 2008), demonstrate attempts by academics and teachers to adapt to the reality of new communication environments.

Each example showcases rich learning experiences that employ digital practices common in society that are not yet fully exploited in all educational contexts.

When we look for literacy practices within the two case studies it is interesting to note what range of literacies can be found. Traditional literacy will be seen in an explicit focus on synthesis and application of discipline knowledge through written language; visual modes will be seen in the attention paid to analysis, synthesis and application of knowledge about design features as well as the requirements of texts on paper and on screen; aural modes will be demonstrated in oral presentations and the use of voice-over and sound effects in digital presentations. Digital literacy will be seen as students create websites, PowerPoint presentations, multimodal texts importing hyperlinked text, animations and video. The technological dimensions are all supported by affordances that provide collaborative contexts encouraging diverse models of social interaction. Technology makes more openings and connections possible through cross-discipline communication via Web 2.0. In all, new ways of learning will be shown to have been created that acknowledge the multiple connections created through technologies. The classroom practices showcased next in the chapter acknowledge the power of split-screen thinking (Claxton 2007) as students simultaneously employ multiple literacies across a range of media, modes and interactive learning opportunities.

Case study 1: a primary classroom

The setting of this case study was a year 6 primary classroom (ages 11–12) in the Australian state of New South Wales (NSW). This case study was part of an ongoing research project (Walsh 2008, 2009) where several primary school teachers included digital technologies in their programmes along with their focus on literacy. The purpose of the study was to consider the way teachers could balance the use of print-based texts with digital texts. All the teachers chose to work with integrated programmes that included two or more curriculum areas. In this case the approach taken by two teachers was to combine their year 6 classes together for a five-week programme that integrated science and English curriculum with the focus topic 'How can we conserve the environment?' Box 1 presents a summary of the teachers' programme.

A range of learning outcomes was occurring through this comprehensive and ambitious programme. The discipline knowledge of science was built up through students investigating the general question 'How can we conserve the environment?' and through researching a related topic and conducting experiments on a specific topic. Students' involvement in the scientific experiments allowed them to explore the impact of humans on the environment and to consider the importance of valuing and conserving the environment for future generations. There were

Box 1. Case study 1: conserving the environment

Students in two year 6 classes worked together as the teachers introduced them to the importance of conservation. All students read a text about the use of garbage and waste consumption, *The Tin Forest* (Ward and Anderson 2003), and were given a number of relevant websites to search related to the effect of human activity on the environment. Then, as a whole class, they developed a mind map for the different kinds of human impact on the environment, e.g. underground water, water salinity, landfill, air pollution, power, ozone depletion/ greenhouse gases and the effect of oil spills.

In groups, students then conducted small experiments related to environmental issues (e.g. measuring the amount of waste from a tap dripping over 24 hours; testing whether oil absorbs in water to consider the effect of oil spillages on the environment) and recorded these findings.

Students' group reports of their specific topic were written and emailed to the teacher and other groups. These reports provided online discussions through a class blog between the teacher and between different groups.

These investigations and reports led to each group of students planning and writing expositions to present their argument for conservation in relation to their particular topic (e.g. water conservation, recycling). In this argument they needed to provide evidence they had obtained from their investigations to support the need for conservation. These expositions were published on the class blog, accompanied by photos and short video clips that showed evidence from their experiments.

As students' knowledge of the topic was extended they were required to create a theme related to their science investigation that would be the focus for a video advertisement about conserving the environment. Students developed a slogan that represented their theme and planned the filming of an advertisement that was designed to show the value of the environment and the importance of conservation.

To understand the structure of an advertisement the teachers took students through the process of deconstructing a familiar television advertisement about coffee. Students were led to examine the advertiser's use of a scenario and persuasive language as well as techniques of filming such as how setting, colour, movement and angles were used. Each group produced their short persuasive film advertisement about conserving the environment.

Programmes such as Movie Maker and Ulead (free multimedia software programs for making and editing videos) were later used by groups to edit their short film with a focus on elements of visual literacy including camera angles and position.

specific aspects of oral language and literacy that were needed by the students while they were investigating these scientific issues. The literacy practices of reading and writing were occurring with print and screen-based texts along with a constant blending with the modes of viewing, writing, talking and listening. This articulation between modes appeared more coherent through the affordances of digital technology. Through considering this case study example, we can examine how multiple literacy practices are occurring within digital communication. Box 2 highlights these differences with the left-hand column showing those traditional print-based practices that usually occur in classrooms and the right-hand column describing differences that reveal multiple literacy practices.

Box 2. Description of literacy practices

'traditional' language and literacy practices ⟵⟶	'multiple' literacy practices
Researching and reading for information about environmental issues and conservation. Learning new concepts and technical vocabulary. Identifying and selecting key ideas.	Viewing and reading on screen, browsing, hyper-linking and selecting relevant sites and information.
At relevant times, teacher modelling and scaffolding of the different text types of report and exposition.	Writing reports on screen for blog, responding to others in blog, uploading files, understanding Web 2.0 software and protocols.
Talking and listening occurring throughout as students worked in groups for experiments, written products and filming.	Producing reports and expositions on screen. Incorporating photographs and short video files into expositions. Viewing, deconstructing and designing of advertisements.
Considering the importance of audience.	Production of 'storyboards' for filming advertisements with use of written text, photos or graphics. Design of setting, characters and camera shots. Understanding of editing process.
	Considering the impact of the digital product on audience.

The descriptions in Box 2 demonstrate that literacy is different when combined with digital technology and, in fact, students can be engaged in multiple literacy practices that are integrated and often interdependent. Reading and viewing occurred with the reading of print as well as screen-based texts, as students were required to search, identify and select relevant information from information books and websites. The students were required to use inferential and critical reading strategies that have always represented important reading skills, but they were required to apply these in a web-based environment, where it is often difficult to choose the most relevant pathways and to evaluate the authenticity of sites. This 'reading on screen' (Bearne *et al.* 2007) can involve the simultaneous viewing and processing of text, images and graphics.

Talking and listening within collaborative group situations were essential aspects of the students' research, experiments and report preparation. These group reports were written, then communicated online for others to read and comment. The writing of both reports and then expositions, with students developing an argument for conservation as a result of their investigations, was scaffolded through different stages of the programme by the teachers. These written texts were produced on screen as well as on paper. Within this new learning environment collaboration took on a new importance for students who were working together to often develop a completed product for an audience. The social dynamics of the classroom were changing, as students cooperated and communicated online as well as in their class groups. While the teachers introduced students cautiously to aspects of social networking through these online tasks, it was revealing to see how instantly students were engaged in communicating in this way. This enthusiasm was a common response through the other case studies in the larger project, and it is difficult to determine whether students' responses were positive because of the novelty of the activities, or whether their responses were more intuitive because of the way similar communication practices now occur in the wider community. Whatever the reason, it has to be acknowledged that digital technologies have contributed to changed social practices that are integral to changed literacy practices.

It is important to comment on the changing nature of writing itself within this case study. As students transferred their written texts onto the screen, they became conscious of the importance of presentation and audience. They were concerned with the polishing of their final product so that arrangement of text on the screen was supplemented by scanned photographs or drawings, with attention to headings and fonts as well as spelling and punctuation. The teachers commented that students were more concerned with these features than they usually were with their writing on paper. One of the teacher's comments reflected the change that they had perceived in the students' engagement with writing compared with previous lessons:

> T: The students were highly motivated by writing when it was combined with the task of producing an exposition in the form of a digital advertisement.

Clearly, students were concerned with the design of their screen-based texts that others would view and comment on. Design is emerging as a significant element of being literate in digital communication environments (Healy 2008;

Kalantzis and Cope 2005), and case study 1 confirms the integral nature of design within the students' work. Design is also a significant feature in the next case study that introduces work completed as part of a collaborative teaching project in a pre-service teacher education programme at an urban university. In some ways the preparation of the tertiary students mirrors what is happening in the primary classrooms above.

Case study 2: a tertiary context

The setting of case study 2 is a Bachelor of Education (BEd) programme in an urban university in NSW, Australia. The university programme prepares students to teach literacy to primary school children. This case study forms part of a collaborative research project in pre-service teacher education in higher education (Simpson 2007; Simpson and Preston 2008) where lecturers in charge of English and science units of study planned cross-disciplinary learning experiences that incorporated the use of ICT for 200 final year BEd students. The purpose of the study was to examine how the explicit scaffolding of literacy practices, within the creation of multimodal texts appropriate for teaching young children about science, could improve students' confidence as teachers of science. Research shows that school science can be improved by attention given to the teaching and exploration of language through the reading and writing of science and the analysis of scientific argument (Osborne 2002: 215). In the study students engaged in practices that incorporated the use of new and traditional literacies into science and English units for one semester. At the start of the semester students were arranged in groups and given a published scientific text on a focus topic for close study. The topics encouraged investigation of ideas within the built environments content strand of the NSW K–6 science syllabus so students would explore how people create, construct, modify and adapt structures for a wide range of purposes. The students were given instruction on how to critique their texts according to the scientific accuracy and grammatical structure as examples of explanation texts.

Box 3 presents a summary of how one group of students worked through the integrated project. Their topic focused on the question 'How do columns support and bear loads?'

The key learning outcomes were designed for the students so that they would meet the NSW Institute of Teachers 2009 accreditation standards of knowing the syllabus content of all the curriculum areas and knowing how to teach it to students (http://www.nswteachers.nsw.edu.au/). The group's focus question 'How do columns support and bear loads?' required students to research accurate scientific information and write an appropriately worded text for their audience. As part of their professional learning, they also need to demonstrate their ability

Box 3. Case study 2: scientific literacies – explaining to primary school children how columns support and bear loads

One group of five students chose to investigate how columns support and bear loads vertically but not horizontally to demonstrate their function in built environments, as the background to developing an explanation text suitable for young children. In their English tutorials they learned about the social purpose, structure, language and visual design features of explanation texts using a rubric drawn up by the lecturers as a guide. The rubric scaffolded students to assess the text in categories such as, for example: identifying statement and explanation sequence, timeless tense, appropriate technical language to label images.

Students collected a range of multimodal scientific explanation texts about columns from books and websites and critiqued them using the same rubric. The critiques of published explanation texts were shared in blogs with the lecturer and other group members. These critiques gave students core knowledge about the content, form and potential design features of the text that they needed to create for their audience. The students also needed to identify the core teaching points in the science topic and then develop new multimodal texts to teach them. For example, the group discovered that columns work on the vertical principle where weight placed on top of the column is evenly distributed throughout the cylindrical shape.

In their science tutorial students used syllabus documents to ascertain which year of primary school would learn about columns and therefore the level of linguistic complexity their written text should incorporate. For example, an indicator for built environments listed for exploration in stage 2 requires primary students to test different structures, make predictions and draw conclusions about the strongest shape for supporting an object or load. In English tutorials the university students matched the syllabus requirements for stage 2. For example, in stage 2 primary students must learn the grammatical features associated with different text types, such as text connectives used to sequence explanations. Through this preparation the students built up their understanding of how English is a core factor in planning for teaching in an integrated approach to develop discipline knowledge within science and technology.

In the next phase of the project students were given some basic instruction in the creation of digital texts using PowerPoint. The students used emails, blogs and other digital communication opportunities to work collaboratively. They were required to embed video, audio, animations, hypertext, written explanations and lesson notes in their new texts. The columns group made use of multimedia software programs to make and edit their own video to demonstrate how the structure of an egg is like a hollow column that can bear weight vertically in an engaging manner for young children.

The group designed their text and lesson sequence as appropriate for young children to meet the strict scientific and linguistic criteria already trialled as well as the new multimodal criteria. For example, their text included causal conjunctions and strategically linked visual and verbal grammar to enhance teaching of scientific concepts. The students uploaded their multimodal learning object for peer feedback. The texts created by the columns group were critiqued by other students in online discussions. Tutors then marked the multimodal texts using the rubrics modelled earlier.

A public display of the texts in the form of a PowerPoint presentation was held. The group justified the design of their multimodal text according to how it suited the content of their explanation focus. Through this process students developed explicit knowledge of how literacy is integral to scientific understanding in the context of teaching their chosen focus area. After revision for corrections, final products were published online in a locked website as a future resource for all the students in the cohort to access.

to integrate technology successfully into their teaching and to support the literacy development of all children through explicit teaching. The two year 4 units of study worked in parallel to integrate learning from the cross-discipline areas of English and science to embed awareness of multiple literacy practices in teaching. The findings of the project demonstrated that this kind of learning improved students' confidence in teaching science and increased their appreciation of literacy and new literacies used in appropriate contexts (Simpson 2007). To discover how multiple literacy practices contributed to that process we will now provide a comparison with print-based practices. Box 4 highlights relationships to those seen in Box 2 above.

As Box 4 shows, the literacy practices in which students became involved were just as diverse as in the primary school context. The descriptions demonstrate that traditional literacy practices became more diverse in nature as they were combined with digital technology. Students needed to integrate multiple literacy practices to participate successfully in each step of the cross-disciplinary project. Reading, writing, talking and listening and viewing opportunities were given with both print and multimodal texts. Students critically analysed existing texts and then designed new texts according to a rubric combining literacy (verbal and visual) and science knowledge. Students were required to: use syllabus documents to identify a topic relevant to a developmental stage, discriminate between accurate and inaccurate scientific information, evaluate appropriate language and visual material (e.g. diagrams in multimodal texts), understand new and technical vocabulary along with the discourse of scientific language, synthesise and apply new knowledge.

The pedagogic decisions on which the project was based encouraged collaborative learning as a result of explicit teaching through the creation of digital multimodal texts. Tertiary students are familiar with social networking in the world outside the university. The research study results show that the inclusion of Web 2.0 interactions in this teaching context supported student learning by creating opportunities for asynchronous communication and building archives of discussions. Talking and listening were stimulated in collaborative chat

Box 4. Description of literacy practices

'traditional' language and literacy practices ⟷	'multiple' literacy practices
Researching and reading for information about columns. Learning new concepts and technical vocabulary. Identifying and selecting key ideas. At relevant times, teacher modelling and scaffolding the text type of explanation. Talking and listening occurring throughout as students worked in groups for lesson planning, text critique and written text production.	Viewing and reading on screen, browsing, hyperlinking and selecting relevant sites and information. Writing reports on screen for blog; responding to others in blog; uploading files; understanding Web 2.0 software and protocols. Producing lesson plans and explanations on screen. Incorporating photographs and short video files into explanations. Viewing, deconstructing and designing new multimodal texts. Production of 'storyboards' using an egg as a column video; explanation made use of written text, photos and graphics. Design of setting, camera shots, voice-over narration. Understanding of editing process. Developing understanding of the importance of audience for age-appropriate scientific texts.

groups and contributed to the development of shared group knowledge. Written texts were developed through the online decision-making processes, which contributed to the production of multimodal explanations. The collaborative process signals a shift towards integrated learning for the coordinators of these two units of study. The intervention was aimed at increasing pre-service teachers' confidence and competence in teaching science in primary school. Students' feedback demonstrates the value they attached to this form of learning:

S1:   I can see how you could really teach scientific concepts through literacy now ... in terms of [concepts such as] the explanation of life cycles and things like that. This kind of work helps to connect learning across the whole scope of sequence of K–6.

In summary, while the students in both research studies were involved in a range of reading and writing print-based activities, these were augmented by the affordances of digital technologies. We have highlighted the multiple literacies that students operated across page and screen. Futures-oriented pedagogy should demonstrate a broad conceptualisation of literacy that allows for 'the effective integration of print literacy and digital literacy (page to screen). It should not involve a choice between the world of the page and the world of the screen – education needs to give attention to both' (Snyder 2008: 167-68). In our case studies reading and viewing occurred on screen as well as with the medium of film and printed books. Writing was extended into published work and arranged with photos and graphics. Aided by digital software programmes, a great deal of the students' work was developed into a video that they designed and edited. Students were engaged in learning about the structure and language for writing particular text-types as well as the structure and design of words with other modes of image or sound. Students were learning the metalanguage of written structures and grammar associated with English along with the metalanguage of digital texts. The case studies show that students shifted in their multiple-literacies competence as they internalised knowledge through their learning experiences (Lo Bianco and Freebody 1997: 84). Further, there was evidence of the importance of social networking within these examples. Even with these two small case studies, there was a distinctive appeal for students to connect and communicate with their peers online.

Conclusion

This chapter commenced by positioning the argument about the nature of literacy at a time when technology has created new forms of communication. Throughout the chapter we have shown how theory has challenged old definitions of literacy, and we have provided examples of how teachers have developed collaborative learning opportunities that incorporate new literate practices. The case studies demonstrate how new technologies are not just being used to create 'old currency' (Yelland *et al.* 2009: 4). Rather, the teachers both in the school and the university were redesigning pedagogy that allowed for the merging of print-based with digital practices of reading and writing. The case studies show that students were dealing with multiple modes and multiple literacies across disciplines in a social learning context.

The case studies illuminate how teachers can incorporate multiple literacy practices in their teaching. However, current policy and curriculum does not always match the work of these forward-thinking educators. There is often a disjunction between what is possible and what is recommended. Future policy makers and curriculum designers need to resolve this dilemma. Although theory and practice have been connected through the examples we have provided, it is clear that a cohesive and comprehensive vision of literacy appropriate for current and future learners has yet to be developed. The world of communication has evolved significantly since the Internet was first used in schools to search sites for information. Now with interactive, multiple authoring and social networking facilities provided by Web 2.0 technologies, new pedagogic possibilities can be utilised in classrooms. The creation of collaborative writing spaces encourages participatory learning through wiki, blogs and other communal sites. To support this evolving context Dyson recommends:

> curricula in which children and teachers use their cultural and symbolic resources to deconstruct and design texts of various modalities, that is, curricula in which they make decisions about the symbolic tools and substance that might suit an ever-widening, evolving network of communicative practices (Dyson in Evans 2004: x).

As it is now recognised that 'new literacies are essential in classrooms so that equal opportunities are offered to all students' (Leu *et al.* in Barone and Wright 2008–2009: 293), the responsibility to provide richer learning opportunities through participatory education increases. Thus the key implication from this chapter is the need for policy makers to embed multiple modes and multiple literacies in the future design of curriculum and pedagogy.

References

Barone, T. and Wright, T. (2008–2009) Literacy instruction with digital and media technologies. *The Reading Teacher* 62 (4): 292-303.

Bearne, E., Clark, C., Johnson, A., Manford, P., Mottram, M. and Wolstencroft, H. (2007) *Reading on Screen Research Report*. United Kingdom Literacy Association.

Carrington, V. (2005) New textual landscapes, information and early literacy. In J. Marsh (ed.) *Popular Culture, New Media and Digital Literacy in Early Childhood*. London: Routledge Falmer.

Claxton, G. (2007) Expanding young people's capacity to learn. *British Journal of Educational Studies* 55 (2): 115-34.

Coiro, J., Knobel, M., Lankshear, C. and Leu, D. (eds.) (2008) *Handbook of Research on New Literacies*. New York: Lawrence Erlbaum Associates.

Comber, B. and Kamler, B. (2005) *Turn-around Pedagogies: Literacy Interventions for At-Risk Students*. Newtown: Primary English Teaching Association.

Cope, B. and Kalantzis, M. (eds.) (2000) *Multiliteracies: Literacy Learning and the Design of Social Futures*. South Yarra: Macmillan.

Evans, J. (ed.) (2004) *Literacy Moves on: Using Popular Culture, New Technologies and Critical Literacy in the Primary Classroom*. London: David Fulton.

Gamse, B., Tepper Jacob, R., Horst, M., Boulay, B., Unlu, F., Bozzi, L. *et al.* (2008) *Reading First Impact Study: Final Study* (No. NCEE 2009-4038). Washington, DC:

National Centre for Education Evaluation and Regional Assistance: Institute of Education Sciences.

Gee, J. (1996) *Social Linguistics and Literacies: Ideology and Discourses*, 2nd edn. London: Taylor & Francis.

Healy, A. (2008) *Multiliteracies and Diversity in Education*. South Melbourne: Oxford.

Kalantzis, M. and Cope, B. (2005) *Learning by Design (2005–2008), ARC Linkage Project*. http://newlearningonline.com/learning-by-design/research/ (accessed 7 June 2009).

Kress, G. (2003) *Literacy in the New Media Age*. London: Routledge Falmer.

Kress, G., Jewitt, C., Ogborn, J. and Tsatsarelis, C. (2001) *Multimodal Teaching and Learning: The Rhetorics of the Science Classroom*. London: Continuum.

Kress, G. and van Leeuwen, T. (2001) *Multimodal Discourse*. London: Routledge.

Lankshear, C., Bigum, C., Durrant, C., Green, B., Honan, E., Morgan, W. *et al.* (1997) *Digital Rhetorics: Literacies and Technologies in Education – Current Practices and Future Directions*. Canberra: DEETYA.

Lankshear, C. and Knobel, M. (2003) *New Literacies: Changing Knowledge and Classroom Learning*. Buckingham: Open University Press.

Livingstone, S. (2008) *Digital Literacies: Tracing the Implications for Learners and Learning*. Bristol: Economic and Social Research Council.

Lo Bianco, J. and Freebody, P. (1997) *Australian Literacies: Informing National Policy on Literacy Education*. Belconnen: Language Australia.

Merchant, G. (2009) Literacy in virtual worlds. *Journal of Research in Reading* 32 (1): 38-56.

National Council of Teachers of English (2007) *21st Century Literacies*. Urbana, IL: National Council of Teachers of English.

National Curriculum Board (2009) *Shape of the Australian Curriculum: English*. Melbourne: National Curriculum Board.

Osborne, J. (2002) Science without literacy: a ship without a sail. *Cambridge Journal of Education* 32 (2): 203-18.

Rose, J. (2009) *Independent Review of the Primary Curriculum: Final Report* (No. DCSF-00499-2009). Nottingham: Department for Children, Schools and Families.

Simpson, A. (2007) Integrating science and literacy: collaborative learning as a preparation for professional behaviour. Paper presented at the AARE, Fremantle, WA.

Simpson, A. and Preston, C. (2008) Developing scientific literacies for the primary school classroom: disciplined by knowledge. Paper presented at the Disciplinarity, Knowledge and Language symposium, University of Sydney.

Snyder, I. (2008) *The Literacy Wars: Why Teaching Children to Read and Write is a Battleground in Australia*. Crows Nest: Allen & Unwin.

Unsworth, L. (2001) *Teaching Multiliteracies across the Curriculum: Changing Contexts of Text and Image in Classroom Practice*. Philadelphia: Open University Press.

Walsh, M. (2008) Worlds have collided and modes have merged: classroom evidence of changed literacy practices. *Literacy* 42 (2): 101-108.

Walsh, M. (2009) Pedagogic potentials of multimodal literacies. In L. Tan Wee Hin and R. Subramanian (eds.) *Handbook of Research on New Media Literacy at the K-12 Level: Issues and Challenges*. Hershey, PA: IGI Global, 32-47.

Ward, H. and Anderson, T. (2003) *The Tin Forest*. Mascot: Koala Books.

Yelland, N., Lee, L., O'Rourke, M. and Harrison, C. (2009) Rethinking pathways to print literacy: a multiliteracies perspective. *Practically Primary* 14 (1): 4-6.

Notes

[1] **Alyson Simpson** is a senior lecturer at the Faculty of Education and Social Work at the University of Sydney. She teaches in undergraduate and postgraduate pre-service teacher programmes and supervises research candidates studying in the area of literacy/English education. Her research projects have examined designs for e-learning and concepts of visual literacy in higher education and primary schools. She is the co-author of *Children's Literature and Computer Based Teaching* (London: Oxford University Press, 2005) and author of *Reading under the Covers: Helping Children to Choose Books* (Newtown: Primary English Teaching Association, 2008).

Maureen Walsh is Professor of Literacy Education and Assistant Head of School in the School of Education (NSW) at Australian Catholic University (ACU). She leads the recently established Literacy Research Hub at ACU, and for some time her research interests and publications have focused on multimodal literacy. Maureen lectures in English curriculum and literacy education programmes. She received an ALTC award in 2009 for Excellence in Teaching in Higher Education and a Carrick Citation in 2006 for creative and sustained contribution to literacy teacher education. Recent publications include 'Pedagogic potentials of multimodal literacy', in L. Tan Wee Hin and R. Subramanian (eds.), *Handbook of Research on New Media Literacy at the K-12 Level: Issues and Challenges* (Hershey, PA: IGI Global, 2009), 32-47; 'Worlds have collided and modes have merged: classroom evidence of changed literacy practices', *Literacy* 42 (2) (2008): 101-108; and 'The "textual shift": examining the reading process with print, visual and multimodal texts', *Australian Journal of Language and Literacy* (2006).

4 Socially responsible literacy education: toward an 'organic relation' to our place and time

Peter Freebody[1]

> The destruction of the past, or rather of the social mechanisms that link one's contemporary experience to that of earlier generations, is one of the most characteristic and eerie phenomena of the late twentieth century. Most young men and women at the century's end grow up in a sort of permanent present lacking any organic relation to the public past of the times they live in (Hobsbawm 1994: 3).

Introduction

There is a productive ambiguity about the term 'social responsibility': What is the significance of the qualifier 'social'? Do we contrast it with other levels of responsibility along a continuum from the individual to the collective – individual, communal, civic, national, ethnic-cultural? Do we contrast it with types of responsibility such as economic, material, ecological, moral or cultural? Does it refer to responsibilities that are legacies from other places or times, such as socio-political debts whereby historically racial minority and disadvantaged communities have been systematically 'excluded from the civic process' by poor-quality educational provision (Ladson-Billings 2006: 7), or to responsibilities that arise from our past neglect or imagined futures to do with equity, competencies, technologies, or ideological challenges? How does social responsibility relate to the task of developing, or perhaps recovering, an 'organic relation' to the places and times around us?

These potential meanings are worth exploring for educators with an interest in literacy and schooling. A socially responsible literacy education programme should lead to socially responsible learners, to the teaching of literacy in socially responsible ways in and out of classrooms, and to an emphasis on the social nature of the benefits of literacy. That is, it should orient us toward a literate society as a goal, making us alert to, and advocates of, the positive, long-term civic consequences that arise from the distribution of literacy capabilities via strong educational programmes.

This chapter outlines some meanings of 'social responsibility' in the area of literacy education. It suggests that the term be taken to lead educators toward reconsidering their students, their own practices, and their educational materials and assessments in two ways: across place (the variety of lived social conditions that they and their students inhabit) and through time (the role of literacy education in connecting their own and their students' past, present and future).

This chapter turns first to the past to examine social responsibility as a key to the connection between literacy and schooling, and then to some available scenarios of futures for schooling, to draw out their differing implications for literacy educators, and the role of knowledge in learning and schooling. A particular focus is the role of literacy education in the acculturation of youngsters into the powerful curricular forms of knowledge and discourse around which secondary education is built. The argument is that students come to engage the specific literacy demands of the various curriculum areas from the middle primary years onward. Their participation in their own secondary schooling and in their further education and training depends crucially on how well they can engage these high-stakes literacy demands. Further, however, their efficacy as citizens who belong when and where they are, and who act effectively with an understanding of that sense of belonging, also relates strongly to their literacy capabilities.

Schooling and 'social responsibility'

Some notion of social responsibility has long been at the heart of Western ideas about schooling. Even a selective scan of the dramatic moments in that history sends us some clear messages that some version of social responsibility is at the heart of why schools are with us, and why the contents and processes of schooling remain under constant scrutiny, debate and change.

Early records of activities that would be recognisable to us as schooling describe the education of boys in Athens in the fifth–fourth century BCE through the processes of 'paideia' – a distinctively Athenian combination of modelling and training in obedience and inquiry. (The available evidence indicates that even the daughters of the elite of the ancient European world were not exposed to education in literacy or rhetoric until the late Roman Republic era, some hundreds of years later; see, e.g., Bonner 1977; Hemelrijk 1999; Rawson 2003.)

The appearance of schools related directly to the ancient Athenians' view of the distinctiveness of their culture (Havelock 1982; Robb 1994; Thomas 1994). Athens at this time was in the process of losing a debilitating war of attrition, in large part of their own making. They were being brought low by the Spartans, a people whom they regarded as very much their political and cultural inferiors. These conditions intensified Athenians' adherence to their ideal of citizenship, in particular the rights of citizens in the operation of their public legal system, bringing with it

> a growing alliance between the alphabet and the law in all its manifestations ... *Full* participation in these institutions – the heart of Athenian citizenship – required minimum craft-literacy (Robb 1994: 139; emphasis in original)

> in 4th century Athens, literacy and formal education were finally allied, a union not to be severed again in Europe ... Traditional, oral institutions ... for so many centuries at the core of the Hellenic paideia – faded into inconsequence (Robb 1994: 183).

Historically, schooling and literacy have often co-emerged. For instance, the first known law mandating schooling was called the Old Deluder Satan Law. In that law the early Puritan communities of North America required, in 1647, that every settlement of 50 or more families have a school with a reading and writing teacher, to 'outwit' the ways of the Evil One by a very specific form of learning. This is part of what it says:

> It being one chief point of that old deluder, Satan, to keep men from the knowledge of Scriptures, as in former times, by keeping them in an unknown tongue ... that learning might not be buried in the graves of our fathers, in church and commonwealth (cited in Monaghan 2005: 37).

Again, the particular sense of a distinctive cultural and, in this case, religious citizenry led these communities toward a specialised form of literacy. But this law was not aimed only at the provision of reading instruction. Right from the start of legally mandated schooling, acting on the world through writing was also a focus of attention:

> Teaching writing, within this context, was to give young men a tool for the attainment of 'learning' in a way that merely teaching reading could not (Monaghan 2005: 38).

Harvard College had been established in 1636, and it was clear that some notion of religion-informed, active and knowledgeable citizenry, again among the young men of the ruling and aspiring classes, was at the heart of the motivation for the law.

The development of such readers and writers, for both ancient Athens and the fledgling Puritan communities of Virginia, was clearly seen as important for the maintenance of their special communal identities. For both the ancient Athenians and the early American Puritans, the Western initiators of the idea of schooling and of its deep connection to literacy, literacy education involved learners knowing their place in a society whose ways were threatened by those around them. For both the individual learner and the collective, knowing this and acting on it through literacy constituted a social responsibility.

These motivations arose from an aspiration to preserve social homogeneity in the face of potential diversity and the diffusion of political, moral or religious commitments that related centrally to identity, belonging and, in the end, survival as a recognisable group. In contemporary pluralistic societies the notion of social responsibility assumes an additional range of meanings. For instance, Australia is a country with about 100 community or migrant languages and about 65 Aboriginal and Torres Strait Islander languages. The family of dialects we call English has a global span and seems in no apparent danger of disappearing or even shrinking in its availability and influence. So how might 'socially responsible' literacy education function in places and times whose futures seem to involve more uncertainty and diversity than ever?

'Social responsibility' and the future

The discourses of 'futuring' – scenario building, projecting, extrapolating, modelling and the rest – have long formed part of educational debates about curriculum, assessment and policy. Innovations are often described as being pulled along by a future that is known to be both imminent and inevitable. But in fact such 'futuring' is an intervention, for better or worse, durable or transient, in the present activities of teachers and students.

The most widely known models of the future of schooling have been provided by the Center for Educational Research and Innovation at the Organization for Economic and Cultural Development (OECD). The OECD has built up three data-based categories encompassing a total of six scenarios for the global future of schools on the basis of trends in its member nations. These are:

1. *Attempting to maintain the status quo*

> 1.1 Powerful bureaucratically administered school systems continue, resistant to deep change, with increasingly stretched resources.

2. *Diverse, dynamic schooling following deep reforms (two forms of 're-schooling')*

> 2.1 Schools become focused learning organisations, substantial investments in a strong knowledge agenda, in a culture of high quality, experimentation, diversity and innovation, with new forms of evaluation and assessment.

> 2.2 Schools become core social centres. Schooling comes to be seen as an effective bulwark against social and cultural fragmentation in society and the family. Curriculum is defined by collective and community tasks.

3. Pursuit of alternatives as systems disband/disintegrate (three forms of 'deschooling')

3.1 The Market Model is radically extended. Governments withdraw from direct involvement in schooling. There is growing diversity of provision. Consumer 'choice' plays a growing role. 'Indicators' and accreditation arrangements displace public monitoring and curriculum regulation. Painful inequalities arise.

3.2 Schools are replaced by learning networks in a 'networked society'. Small group, home schooling and individualised arrangements become widespread.

3.3 Teacher exodus and system meltdown occur following waves of crises of teacher shortages. A vicious circle of retrenchment, conflict and emergency strategies spurs radical innovation and change.

These, especially the favoured scenarios (2.1 and 2.2, even though OECD does not explicitly express favouritism), all have distinct implications for literacy education. Scenarios 2.1 and 2.2 diverge on the matter of the centrality of knowledge versus community network and building, with corollaries for the localisation versus portability of school-based knowledge and literacy capabilities. That is, the contrast between 2.1 and 2.2 entails a radically different role for access to specialised knowledge, with implications for citizens' agency and participation in complex social and political decisions.

As a recent example, a 'foundation for the future' is spelled out in some detail in terms of skills, dispositions and values in the Australian *National Declaration on Educational Goals for Young Australians* (Ministerial Council on Education, Employment, Training and Youth Affairs, MCEETYA 2008: 5), which asserts that, from their experiences in school, youngsters:

> should have the essential skills in literacy and numeracy and are creative and productive users of technology, especially ICT
>
> are creative, innovative and resourceful
>
> have a sense of optimism about their lives and the future – are enterprising, show initiative and use their creative abilities
>
> develop personal values and attributes such as enterprise, honesty, resilience, empathy and respect for others.

In such documents it is generally clear that, to fulfil their responsibilities, educators, educational institutions and educational systems need to orient to these far-reaching aspects of human behaviour, feeling, thought and moral disposition. The reach of these aspirations for a schooled-literate citizenry (ICT aside) has remained undiminished since fourth-century BCE Athens and the Old Deluder Satan Law.

It is striking how confident are assertions about the educational goals that will provide a platform for youngsters for the new century, whichever century it has been. But is it a warranted confidence, and how might we know that, one way or another? In terms of our interests, how can we reflect on what it actually means to discuss the features of a literacy education programme that might prepare young people to live effectively in the twenty-first century?

We could start with a thought experiment to give us a sense of how close our imaginings might be: move back in time a century, knowing what we now know about what lay in wait for the youngsters in school in 1909, say, born around 1904, and ask the question 'How could we improve our literacy education, or our education more generally, to prepare young people to live in the twentieth century?' This must be easier because we have some idea about what lies in wait and, with benefit of hindsight, we should be able to tailor a 'futures-oriented' schooling experience.

What lay in wait for the kindergarten class of 1909? Here are some events conventionally named in textbooks: the First World War was a few years away, as was the Russian Revolution, the Treaty of Versailles stipulating that Germany may not remilitarise, Germany's remilitarisation, the Great Depression, Japan's attack on Manchuria and China, the Second World War, Hiroshima, Dada, the Chinese Revolution, the cold war, television, Korea, Vietnam on daily television, the Balkans, the Internet, Rwanda, holes in the ozone layer, and so on.

But these are the events; what of the changing conditions of life, the deep sea changes that these events reflected: suburbanisation, flight and mass tourism, telecommunications, Surrealism, mass migration, digitisation, the massification of extended education in the West, civil rights, the financialisation of everything, feminism, iPods, ecological deterioration, global warming, and so on? For many, but by no means all, the world was almost completely remade, and yet still contained brutalities and 'cleansings' whose scale and intensity would have been sadly familiar to our prehistoric ancestors.

Those of our kindergarten class of 1909 who made it to their ninety-seventh birthdays would have watched the planes fly into the skyscrapers on 9/11 on television. Perhaps they reflected that the Wright brothers first took to the air just a few months before they themselves were born, and that they read about it much later in the newspapers.

That kind of challenge, then and probably no less now, reminds us of the well-known quip by Woody Allen: 'If you want to make God laugh, just tell him your plans for the future'. It reminds us that we face the future with skimpy resources: our past in one hand and our optimism in the other.

With the benefit of hindsight, what can we say about the social responsibilities of educators in 1909 to their youngsters? What were the 'essential skills in literacy and numeracy', the 'productive uses of technology'? What counted as creative, innovative, resourceful and optimistic people? And what of the 'honesty, resilience, empathy and respect for others' needed in the century that Eric Hobsbawm (1994) has famously described as 'the age of extremes'?

How imaginable were young people's future needs in 1909? How educationally actionable were our glimpses of them? Could we, to put it bluntly, have actually got anywhere near designing schooling that would prepare youngsters in 1909 for what lay ahead of them?

Contemplating what we would have done with all this hindsight immediately draws our attention to notions of literacy teaching and learning that extend well beyond competence in the minimal technical aspects of managing and producing everyday texts. The twentieth century was to call for some form of extended schooling into adolescence that offered the chance of bringing some competent appreciation of the bodies of knowledge that were growing and growing in importance in ways that were simply unimaginable to educators a century ago. Across both place and time, imagining the social responsibilities of literacy educators necessarily confronts us with the institutionally and culturally high-stakes literacy demands that face young learners as they approach knowledge in its curricular forms. Apocalyptic wars, economic crashes, technology and the deep sea changes in human social organisation notwithstanding, the twentieth century could rightly be called the age of knowledge. In that century it was firmly institutionalised in centres of teaching and learning, and fuelled and disseminated by mass printing and new communication technologies.

Literacy in and for school

For students the looming motivation for a socially responsible education comes down to the future that faces them immediately in school and to the consequences, for their own uncertain futures, of how well they can display mastery of various forms of literacy capabilities. From the perspective of a literacy educator, it is clear that the kind of work to which literacy is put begins to diversify in the middle and upper primary years, and to have developed into recognisably curriculum-specific forms by the early secondary years. It is now well documented that curriculum-specific literacy demands need to continue to be developed through the secondary years, regardless of how successful primary school literacy teaching has been (e.g., Christie and Derewianka 2008).

This recognition is reflected in the slogan evident in many curriculum statements to the effect that 'every teacher is a teacher of literacy'. Most curriculum framework documents nowadays emphasise that literacy learning is not complete by year 3 or 4, and that middle and secondary school students need to continue to develop the literacy resources for learning successfully across the various disciplines that underpin the school curricula. The question arises, therefore, as to why, in classrooms, curriculum development offices, assessment regimes and school systems at large, most professional educators need to act as if these propositions are either wrong or irrelevant. These actions have consequences: curriculum-specific literacy difficulties are being mistaken, every day, for a lack of either academic aptitude or effort, and, thereby, a lot of potential curricular aptitude goes unrecognised, and a lot of important knowledge untouched.

David Olson, in a widely cited remark, asserted roundly that 'schooling is a matter of mediating the relationship between children and the printed text' (Olson 1977: 66). Of course, lessons recognisable as teaching and learning in literacy occur daily across the curriculum areas in schools. In early schooling these are named reading, writing or language arts lessons. In them we see a number of features (following Baker and Freebody 1989; Freebody with Chan 2009):

- teachers generally establish specific social processes for the lesson around reading or writing practices, for example, routines and pro-cedures for turning pages, naming letters and sounds, read aloud individually or in round robins, and so on;
- teachers generally mediate what students should do and what they should think in relation to the text, providing an interpretation of the text, including aspects of pictures, orienting students toward particular readings and interpretations, and so on;
- teachers and students generally engage in initiation-response-evaluation exchanges around readings of texts (Mehan 1979), with the teacher managing and redirecting interpretations, and the students responsible for providing possible answers.

It is in social mediation practices, collectively conducted, that students are inducted into ways of thinking and talking as they read and about what they have read, in ways that are adequate to the setting in which they are reading. When we turn to teacher–student interactions in the first year of schooling, we find students acculturated into forms of social responsibility, those relating to turn-taking and answering in classrooms, paying close attention to the teacher's interpretations of texts, including those displayed by sequences of questions. These social respon-sibilities, and how to learn them through everyday interactions (Heap 1991), remain operational for the students' stay in school.

Do such practices hold in the secondary years, or are students expected to be independent readers of the texts they encounter across the curriculum areas? In considering whether or not the slogan 'every teacher is a teacher of literacy' is an exhortation or a simple statement of fact, we can jump forward ten years to a year 11 biology lesson (excerpts from research project, Freebody with Chan 2009). In terms of some of the features illustrated above, is this a literacy lesson? In the excerpts below, students are reading from a handout on the structure and functions of roots and rhizomes. We can see that:

- the teacher establishes reading practices as he develops curriculum knowledge around the text:[2]

t   Now we need to look at root structure cause I want to look at this surface area to volume ratio um and look at an example in plants (.) how it works. Can you please read for us^ ROOT STRUCTURE. Nathal could you read for us. Thank you (2) ROOTS ARE ESSENTIAL V Everyone's with us^ we need to have a look at this V. Go for it.

s-N ROOTS ARE ESSENTIAL PLANT ORGANS. THEY ANCHOR THE PLANT IN THE GROUND AND ABSORB WATER AND MINERALS FROM THE SOIL. THESE MINERALS ARE THEN TRANSPORTED THROUGHOUT THE PLANT …

- the teacher inserts initiation-response-evaluation exchanges into the round robin reading:

s   … LIKE OTHER PARTS OF THE PLANT, ROOTS ARE COVERED IN EPIDERMIS, BUT THE EPIDERMIS DOES NOT HAVE A WAXY LAYER SINCE THIS WOULD//

t   //Why doesn't, sorry, stop there. Why doesn't it have a waxy layer like the leaf^ Please, Mischa^

s-M That's- if it's waxy the water would be able to//

t   //Good but what's the point of having a waxy cuticle on top of a leaf^ though

s   It keeps the water in, it stops it evaporating V

t   yes, go on …

- the teacher focuses the cognitive work of the reading by providing a hierarchy of importance in the information shown in the text and elaborates and gives commentary on the text:

s   um MANY PLANTS … DEPEND ON A MUTUALLY BENEFICIAL SYMBIOTIC ASSOCIATION WITH FUNGI … THE ROOTS, HOWEVER, BECOME INFECTED WITH A FUNGUS … FORMING A MY- (.)

t   It's a condition. Don't worry about it. Yep. Keep going.

s   … THE FUNGUS OBTAINS IMPORTANT ORGANIC COMPOUNDS SUCH
      AS SUGARS AND AMINO ACIDS. IN RETURN, THE FUNGUS GREATLY
      INCREASES THE ABSORPTION OF WATER AND MINERALS BY THE
      PLANT.

t   Highlight that. That's the key idea of this whole article is there's symbiotic
      relationships in which both are benefitting. The fungus gets sugars from the plant
      and the plant increases its surface area for absorption of minerals. Yes um keep
      going please

s   ALSO, THE FUNGUS OFTEN PROVIDES CERTAIN GROWTH
      SUBSTANCES … PROTECTION AGAINST ATTACK BY MICRO-
      ORGANISMS.

t   Good because the fungus, you can also almost call it an aleopathy as well because it
      secretes substances that don't allow other microorganisms to infect the plant
      because it's protecting its food source basically. Keep going.

This is an everyday round robin reading lesson with year 11 students who are, it
seems, fully literate in the technical, basic sense of that expression, and yet who
are co-operating with the teacher's interventions into their reading, interventions
that directly parallel what we find in year 1 reading lessons:

- teachers' interventions connect new knowledge to earlier knowledge
  and to subsequent learning, and to what they know common-sensically
  about the world;
- teachers actively and explicitly structure a hierarchy of importance
  through questioning and through direct statements of importance;
- and teachers and students focus on content and conceptual understanding from the text within a clear social, interactional framework
  for the conduct of the reading.

At the same time, even from this brief contrast, we can see that literacy in the
secondary school can entail more than a literacy lesson in year 1 in that:

- various forms of texts are used as sources of curriculum knowledge;
- students are apprenticed into highly specific ways of reading these
  texts, and using them for further curriculum-specific learning and for
  the creation of new texts;
- curricular knowledge is mediated by how students recontextualise
  their everyday understandings;
- and secondary students are more likely to be held accountable for the
  curricular knowledge rather than for the processes and routines of the
  reading/interpretation lessons themselves.

As a further example, in a year 11 music lesson in which students were asked to analyse a piece of music (a Pavane) and compare its features with another (an Estampie). They listened to music, read from a score, discussed the comparison in small groups, and finally wrote a description, structuring their descriptions and interpretations around musical elements such as rhythm, texture, phrase structure and so on (excerpts from research project, Freebody, Bahr, Wright and Allender forthcoming). The teacher framed the activity like this:

> t   just freely analyse it … just do it as if an alien landed from outer space and you're trying to describe to them what a Pavane is like. What would you tell them? That's what I'm asking you to do. But you need your music beside you to help you.

Students needed to bring to bear sensory experience, theory and technical knowledge in describing what they heard (that is, not just 'hear-and-say' common-sensically); the teacher needed to guide the students toward articulating their hearings and understandings through the logic of the discourses of music. To do this, teachers and students engaged in regular movement back and forth between everyday and specialised, discipline-specific language. Figure 1 (from Freebody with Chan 2009) shows how this shuttling works for a small sample of the lesson.

By senior secondary school the students' developing literacy capabilities take the less immediately obvious form of working back and forth between kinds of technical terminology and registers that are characteristic of the textual forms of a specific curriculum area, even if a written text is not immediately present in the activity itself. In inducting students into curriculum-specific forms of knowledge, teachers interact with them in and out of these forms, in a sense shuttling between curricular and everyday forms of expression (Gibbons 2002; Hammond 1990).

The argument here is that a crucial aspect of socially responsible literacy education calls for an engagement with knowledge in its distinctive patterns and structures. This responsibility clearly applies to students; it has been less force-fully named as the responsibility of literacy educators, designers of curriculum and assessment regimes, teacher educators and researchers. One observation, so clear it is rarely even made, arises from the last 40 years of theorising and researching in and around literacy education: research, professional development and theoretical debate in the area of the curriculum literacies in the secondary school years lag decades behind other areas of literacy education. This is in spite of the fact that reading and especially writing in the high school years are clearly the highest stakes activities for students. The thousands of research projects and papers on the acquisition of early reading, the countless reviews of this vast and diverse literature, the endless media attention it receives, the commercial market-place that has grown up around it, and the Byzantine debates on phonology, pho-nemics, automaticity, rime, rhyme, synthesis and analysis, and all the rest, have

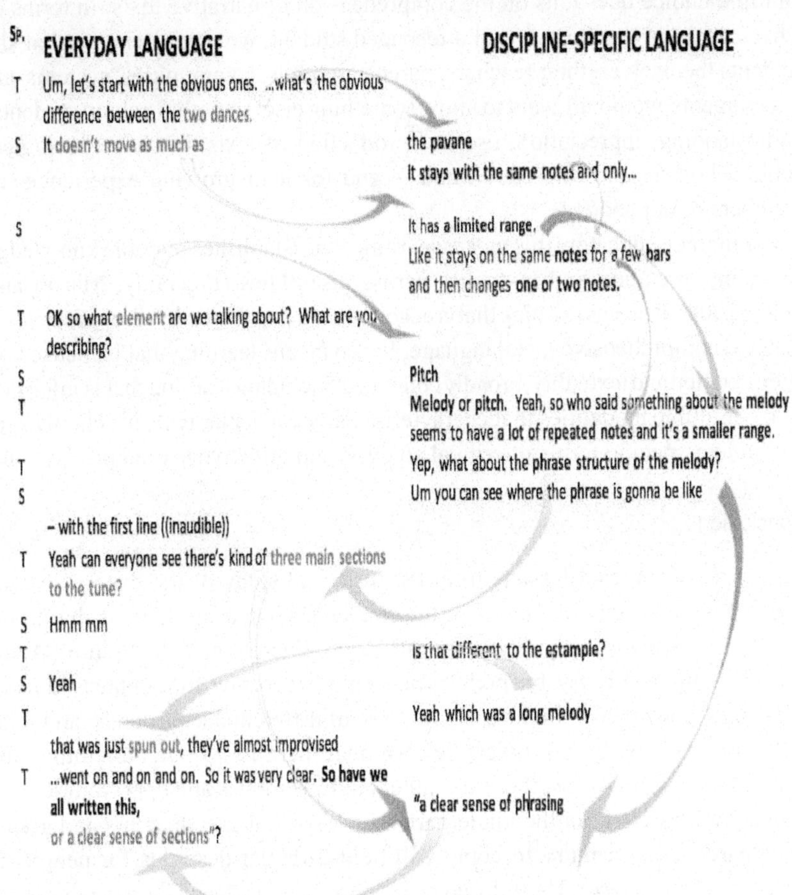

Figure 1. Instances of shuttling between everyday and specialised registers in a year 11 music lesson

given early-reading teachers a rich basis for the professional choices with which they are faced. In contrast, the secondary teacher of any curriculum area will find, with a few exceptions, only limited resources and generally a thin research base (exceptions being Christie 2002, Christie and Misson 1998 and Rush *et al.* 2007).

The standardised, jurisdiction-wide testing currently conducted in many countries for the most part reflects this comparative theoretical and empirical neglect. National literacy testing in the secondary years currently conducted in

Australia, for instance, focuses on low-stakes practices such as answering multiple-choice questions on the comprehension of narrative texts. In terms of what counts in the daily life of a teenaged student, we would expect that the students themselves, their teachers, parents, schools, communities, systems and governments would all want to know something else: something about students' understanding, appreciation, use and production of texts that have ecological validity both in and for school, and in and for their growing experiences as members of our society.

For literacy educators this means learning that establishes portable knowledge about interpretation and textuality across disciplines (Freebody, Martin and Maton 2008). It means learning that is accompanied and driven by an appropriately rich and comprehensive metalanguage. It also means learning that is focused on interpretation and textuality, broadly construed, including learning that is informed by the multiple modalities that characterise daily curricular texts in schools, and curriculum-specific forms of critical analysis and effective textual production.

Conclusion

One of the significant lessons from the historical study of the experiences of young people in school in terms of the challenges that await them is that those experiences will be vastly diverse (Graff 1995). There is no 'The Future'. At all periods of human history, but perhaps never more than now, the contrasts in ways of living among people in different regions, of different backgrounds, and with different levels of access indicate clearly that there is no singular future for youngsters in school now; there are rather multiple threats and opportunities. As for the youngsters from the kindergarten of 1909, our grandparents and great-grandparents, the century to come will hold different destinies for people in different circumstances. These different futures are significant for literacy educators, because their students may not operate with the same optimistic connection between school success in literacy and across the curriculum as do they themselves.

Teese and Lamb (2009), for example, have shown growing discrepancies in academic achievement in schools between students from differing socio-economic levels. The discrepancies are also reflected in the increasingly less frequent choice by students from lower socio-economic levels of the traditional, longer, more discipline-based subjects in high school. Teese and Lamb argue that this is because many of these students and their parents know that 'for those students who have been less successful in the compulsory years, there are real dangers in how the curriculum is structured and in how courses or subjects are designed' (Teese and Lamb 2009: 14). Understanding curriculum areas as threats to some students can come only from a socially responsible grasp of schooling, one that orients educators to helping those students as they confront those threats in the middle and secondary years.

The economic and civil responsibilities of literacy educators include developing a well-trained and literate citizenry and workforce. For a view of their distinctly social responsibilities, however, they can look to their professional forebears, who worked in often unfamiliar, and sometimes destitute and threatening conditions. The efforts and sacrifices of those past educators make it now possible to turn attention to providing all learners with access to knowledge that can enhance their competence, their agency, and their organic relation to the places and times they inhabit.

References

Baker, C.D. and Freebody, P. (1989) *Children's First School Books: Introductions to the Culture of Literacy*. Oxford: Basil Blackwell.

Bonner, S.F. (1977) *Education in Ancient Rome: From the Elder Cato to the Younger Pliny*. Los Angeles: University of California Press.

Christie, F. (2002) The development of abstraction in adolescence in subject English. In M. Schleppegrell and C. Colombi (eds.) *Developing Advanced Literacy in First and Second Languages: Meaning with Power*. Hillsdale, NJ: Erlbaum, 45-66.

Christie, F. and Derewianka, B. (2008) *School Discourse: Learning to Write across the Years of Schooling*. London and New York: Continuum.

Christie, F. and Misson, R. (eds.) (1998) *Literacy and Schooling*. London: Routledge.

Dewey, J. (1916) *Democracy and Education*. New York: Macmillan.

Freebody, P. with Chan, E. (2009) Bridges and divides in high stakes curriculum knowledge, language, and literacy in the classroom. Keynote address to the combined National Conference of the Australian Literacy Educators Association and the Australian Association for Teachers of English, Hobart, Tasmania.

Freebody, P., Bahr, N., Wright, T. and Allender, T. (forthcoming) *Disciplinarity and Classroom Practice: Epistemological Issues in the Analysis and Improvement of Teaching and Learning*. Australian Research Council project.

Freebody, P., Hedberg, J.G., Nichols, K., van Rooy, W., van Bergen, P. and Chan, E. (forthcoming) *Transforming the Technologies and Modalities of Learning: The Case of the New Life Sciences in Secondary Schooling*. Australian Research Council project.

Freebody, P., Martin, J.R. and Maton, K. (2008) Talk, text, and knowledge in cumulative, integrated learning. *Australian Journal of Language and Literacy* 31: 188-201.

Gibbons, P. (2002) *Scaffolding Language, Scaffolding Learning: Teaching Second Language Learners in the Mainstream Classroom*. Portsmouth, NH: Boynton/Cook.

Graff, H.J. (1995) *Conflicting Paths: Growing up in America*. Cambridge, MA: Harvard University Press.

Hammond, J. (1990) Is learning to read and write the same as learning to speak? In F. Christie (ed.) *Literacy for a Changing World*. Hawthorn, Victoria: ACER, 26-53.

Havelock, E. (1982) *The Literate Revolution in Greece and its Cultural Consequences*. Princeton, NJ: Princeton University Press.

Heap, J. (1991) A situated perspective on what counts as reading. In C.D. Baker and A. Luke (eds.) *Towards a Critical Sociology of Reading Pedagogy*. Amsterdam and Philadelphia, PA: John Benjamins.

Hemelrijk, E.A. (1999) *Matrona Docta: Educated Women in the Roman Elite from Cornelia to Julia Domna*. London: Routledge.

Hobsbawm, E. (1994) *The Age of Extremes: The Short Twentieth Century, 1914–1991*. London: Michael Joseph.

Ladson-Billings, G. (2006) From the achievement gap to the education debt: understanding achievement in U.S. Schools. (2006 Presidential Address, American Educational research Association). *Educational Researcher* 35: 3-12.

Mehan, H. (1979) *Learning Lessons: Social Organization in the Classroom*. Cambridge, MA: Harvard University Press.

Ministerial Council on Education, Employment, Training and Youth Affairs, MCEETYA (2008) *National Declaration on Educational Goals for Young Australians*. Canberra: MCEETYA. http://www.curriculum.edu.au/verve/_resources/Draft_National_Declaration_on_Educational_Goals_for_Young_Australians.pdf (accessed 1 July 2009).

Monaghan, E.J. (2005) *Learning to Read and Write in Colonial America*. Boston: University of Massachusetts Press.

Olson, D.R. (1977) The languages of instruction: the literate bias of schooling. In R.C. Anderson, R.J. Spiro and W.E. Montague (eds.) *Schooling and the Acquisition of Knowledge*. Hillsdale, NJ: Erlbaum, 65-89.

Rawson, B. (2003) *Children and Childhood in Roman Italy*. Oxford: Oxford University Press.

Robb, K. (1994) *Literacy and Paideia in Ancient Greece*. Oxford: Oxford University Press.

Rush, L.S., Eakle, A.J. and Berger, A. (2007) *Secondary School Literacy: What Research Reveals for Classroom Practice*. Urbana, IL: National Council of Teachers of English.

Teese, R. and Lamb, S. (2009) Low achievement and social background: patterns, processes and interventions: a discussion paper. The University of Melbourne, Centre for Post-Compulsory Education and Lifelong Learning.

Thomas, R. (1994) Literacy and the city-state in archaic and classical Greece. In A.K. Bowman and G. Woolf (eds.) *Literacy and Power in the Ancient World*. Cambridge: Cambridge University Press.

Notes

[1]   **Peter Freebody** is a professorial research fellow based in the Faculty of Education and Social Work at the University of Sydney. His research interests include literacy education and its relationship to digital technologies, disciplinary knowledge and socio-economic disadvantage. His books include: *Literacy Education in Schools: Research Perspectives from the Past, for the Future* (Melbourne: Australian Council for Educational Research, 2007); *Qualitative Research in Education: Interaction and Practice* (London: Sage, 2003). He has contributed numerous invited entries in international handbooks and encyclopaedias on literacy, critical literacy and research methodology, and has served on numerous state and national advisory groups in the area of literacy education and curriculum design.

2   Transcription conventions used in this chapter:

t means teacher speaking
s means student speaking
s-X means students named in talk, initial X, speaking
UPPER CASE indicates that these words are being read.
^ and V indicate, respectively, strong upward and downward intonation
(x) means pause for x seconds
(.) means brief but noticeable pause
// means interrupted turn at talk

5 Literacy and the Arts

Robyn Ewing[1]

The Arts are the window to the soul …
(George Bernard Shaw in Gire 1996: 41)

Introduction

This chapter begins with the assertion that an Arts-led literacy curriculum is imperative if today's students are to leave school with a sense of their own identity and a place within their social world, along with the creative and flexible literacy skills needed for life in the twenty-first century. Embedding the Arts in formal literacy learning contexts enables educators to enhance students' imaginative capacities. This is central to student learning because, as Wordsworth (in Egan 1992: 25) proclaimed, imagination is 'reason in her most exalted mood'. Kieran Egan's Imaginative Research in Education (IERG) website reminds us that imagination is 'the ability to think of the possible, not just the actual, it is the source of invention, novelty and flexibility in human thinking … it greatly enhances rational thought'.

Initially this chapter provides a definition of how the term 'the Arts' should be understood for this discussion. A brief justification for the role of the Arts in imaginative learning follows, specifically in relation to the literacy curriculum and drawing on a range of relevant research and literature. Finally, two recent exemplars of Arts-led literacy programmes with primary students demonstrate the power of such curriculum experiences.

Defining the Arts

The 'Arts' is used throughout this chapter as a shorthand term for a complex group of creative disciplines including storytelling, literature, dance, drama, visual arts, music, film and media. Each of these is a discrete and distinctive discipline or field of knowledge in its own right, but there are some important resonances that make their coming together logical. Award-winning Australian author and illustrator Tan (2008) recently defined 'art' as the transformation of an idea, subject or concept by an artist. All forms of the creative arts are inextricably linked to our imaginations and involve play, experimentation, exploration and aesthetics or the artistic shaping (or to use Tan's word, 'transforming') of the body or other media to bring together emotions as well as personal, sensory and intellectual experiences into some kind of whole or integrated statement.

In Australia, while literature, music and visual arts have long been part of the intended school curriculum in each state, literature is usually included in the English curriculum and is often omitted in discussions about the Arts. Authentic literary texts including narratives, poems and picture books should be an essential component of classrooms where children are learning to be literate. These class-rooms are, unfortunately, often dominated by texts in which the vocabulary is controlled or levelled and the syntax oversimplified because these kinds of texts are thought to be more accessible to emergent readers. Such practices often disengage children from learning to read. The language of quality literature is artistic, evocative and expressive, rich and meaningful on many levels. If images are embedded in the text they too should be interpretive rather than merely supportive of the written text. Keifer (1995: 6) terms picture books 'unique arts objects' because they bring together images and ideas that engage students holistically with a story. Interpretive and evocative texts are often multilayered and can therefore be enjoyed many times over by readers of different ages and stages (Ewing, Miller and Saxton 2008).

For many children, despite the importance of the aesthetic in their early play, once they begin school, experience of Arts activities remains relegated to the extracurricular part of their lives. Some teachers focus primarily on literacy and numeracy activities. Others do not feel confident about integrating Arts strategies in their planned teaching and learning experiences. Given their importance, it is unfortunate that Arts experiences can become marginalised or only within reach of children from more affluent families, on the 'sidelines of critical conversations' (Hoffman Davis 2005: 12).

O'Toole (2008), a leading Australian Arts educator, outlines three distinct approaches to the formal teaching of the Arts:

1. appreciation of our Arts heritage because the Arts are an important expression or representation of a particular culture or tradition;
2. preparation of those who are identified as having potential performance and/or design skills for a future career in the Arts;
3. expression and communication through the Arts for all rather than only those identified as possessing particular talent or skill in a particular Arts discipline.

Australian Arts syllabi have usually incorporated creating, communicating, appreciating and some performing or presenting components. While different art forms should be taught in their own right, this chapter specifically examines the role that the Arts can play in pedagogy across the curriculum and particularly in literacy learning. The next section briefly examines the importance of the Arts in learning across the curriculum.

The Arts and learning

The enhancement of learning through the Arts is not a recent phenomenon. The study of music was recommended by Greek philosophers more than two thousand years ago as a way to enhance the soul. Dewey (1989) readily acknowledged the artistic qualities of young children's play and its foundation for their learning. These understandings have been extended and elaborated in a multiplicity of scholarly research and writing through the work of many educators (including, for example, Lowenfeld 1947; Slade 1954; Piaget 1962; Read 1964; Vygotsky 1971; Abbs 1987; Heathcote and Bolton 1995; Greene 1995). Egan (1988) links the ancient art of storytelling with enhancing students' learning across the curriculum. In a similar vein, Eisner (2005) argues that, at least post-Renaissance, it is often assumed that the Arts enrich our lives through the engagement of our emotions (and there is no doubt that they do). He suggests that while abstract intellectual activity has traditionally been seen to be more the province of the sciences, there is compelling evidence that the Arts are also pivotal for the development of the intellect.

In his important report for the Blair government in the United Kingdom, creativity and Arts advocate Robinson (1999) suggested that too often a hierarchy of subjects puts mathematics and science at the top of the school curriculum and humanities and the Arts at the bottom. He emphasised that creativity and literacy are of equal importance to mathematics and suggested that fostering creativity would enable students to interpret and appreciate the real meaning of being literate. Similarly Egan (e.g., 1988, 2007) has argued consistently for more than two decades that our neglect of children's imaginations in twentieth-century Western curricula has dulled their intellectual excitement. It is now widely documented (e.g., Deasy 2002; Bamford 2006; Fiske 1999, Catterall *et al.* 1999) that those students whose learning is embedded in the Arts (often called 'high arts students' in the United States) achieve better grades and test scores, are less likely to drop out, rarely report boredom, are more involved in community service and have a more positive self-concept than their counterparts who experience learning with little or no focus on the Arts.

There are many examples of research that demonstrate how particular art forms enhance students' learning. A few are briefly cited here. Over the last 15 years neuroscientific research has confirmed the interrelationship of good emotional function and learning. For example Damasio (1994) and Williams and Gordon

(2007) demonstrate that the human brain must feel comfortable or safe before it can engage in explorative, creative or problem-solving processes. Collaborative strategies common in creative dance and drama activities have been shown to achieve an increase in synchrony and associated bonding. Such cooperation encourages the breaking up of old, often rigid patterns of thinking and behaviour (Freeman 1995) which potentially increases the learner's ownership of and engagement in new learning activities. Children who studied music over at least a year scored better on intelligence tests as well as school grades compared with their counterparts who did not (Schellenberg and Peretz 2008). Those who had drama lessons instead, however, performed more highly on measures that examined social skills. Brice Heath (2000) quotes research suggesting that moving from physical enactment or embodiment of an idea or event to a visual representation and then to written representation extends and develops children's neural circuitry. Imaginative writing has been shown to be greatly enhanced through the use of process drama (O'Neill 1995) strategies (e.g., Crumpler and Schneider 2002; McNaughton 1997). A successful museum education programme used visual works of art to build students' qualitative reasoning (Eisner 2002; Dewey 1989) giving them strategies to better attend to perceptual detail, explore the effect of art works on their emotions and make their own interpretations. This programme focused on developing students' tools for discussing art rather than the more traditional art-making focus (Siegesmund 2005). The Arts can therefore offer critical, quality pedagogy across the curriculum as well as in their individual discipline areas.

Despite its singularity, the term 'literacy' should not imply that it is a single global skill. All students must be able to engage in, understand and analyse an increasing range of manipulations and applications of language and image. In chapter 3 Simpson and Walsh argued that traditional print literacy is no longer sufficient in the information or knowledge age we now inhabit. Understanding the information we receive from computers, mobile phones, blogs, photographs, paintings, billboards and podcasts (to name a few) means that we must be able to intelligently sift the myriad of information that bombards us daily. Arts processes facilitate the selection, analysis, reflection and interpretation of information, at the same time enabling us to become more aware of our own social and cultural biases. In addition, Arts experiences allow all students to take part regardless of their initial linguistic abilities. Students' social skills including active listening and the ability to work collaboratively are also enhanced.

As well as developing our minds, the Arts enable us to convey meaning through less traditional uses of our language resources (consider what the language of poetry makes possible as one example). Given the constant and accelerating change that is part of our lives today, and the escalating literacy demands placed on all learners, the ability to think and communicate creatively in multiple ways is increasingly important. Yet the current focus around measurement of technical literacy skills through multiple-choice tests have contributed greatly to an over-valuing of these aspects of literacy because they are easier and cheaper to measure. Teachers also often feel constrained or under some pressure to teach to such tests. While testing is arguably more efficient, economical and precise about what it measures than some Arts-based assessments, it fails to assess how students generate meaning from texts or how they analyse and interrogate the deep meanings of texts. Multiple-choice comprehension questions restrict or narrow our ability to make the links between real-life literacy and communication (Mills 2008).

Recent research into the structure of the brain and how it operates supports the view that decoding of letter–sound relationships is only one part of literacy learning. On its own, decoding does not create the meaning and understanding that is essential to be critically literate. Critical literacy is defined here as the ability to understand and make meanings that penetrate literal or surface interpretations of texts coupled with the ability to think about the implications for different contexts (after Freire 1985 and Shor 1987). When we read and share stories, relating them to our own experiences and examining the implications for our own lives, we often come to greater understandings about ourselves. These kinds of opportunities with literature help form our personal and social identities and can enable us to escape from the rigidity of these identities. Narrative provides order to our experience and helps us to understand realities (Bruner 1986).

The same research emphasises the importance of predictive and meaningful learning experiences coupled with integrative approaches to learning so that real-world connections, higher order thinking and deep learning can challenge students to think beyond the surface meaning of any text (see, for example, the excellent summary of current research understandings in this field by Strauss, Goodman and Paulson 2009). These findings parallel Freire's (1985: 43-65) early work about the paucity and inappropriate use of contrived reading materials: in texts written with controlled vocabulary and syntax the learning processes are limited because they remain in the hands of the writers and teachers rather than in those of the learners, and a 'culture of silence' is perpetuated. He argued that those who are oppressed are not able to engage actively or creatively in the learning process and remain only marginally involved in learning to be literate (1986: 60-95).

The importance of student engagement in the learning process itself and ownership of the learning cannot be overemphasised. Many children opt out of literacy and other formal learning activities because they cannot see the relevance for their own lives. Too often learning in schools is very different from learning that happens in children's everyday worlds. Ensuring that Arts experiences are programmed with literacy activities can:

- facilitate students' involvement in the literacy experience helping them make links with their own knowledge and experiences;
- enable a range of possible meanings to be explored and represented;
- provide opportunities for students to reflect on the purposes of the text and how choices about its structure have contributed to communicating these purposes;
- apply understandings to their own personal context or other contexts.

The next section provides two examples from several related Arts and literacy projects currently underway in a number of Sydney schools. Each has embedded the Arts as critical pedagogy within the literacy programme. Each project provides the potential for the achievement of the points listed above.

The Arts as critical pedagogy: recent classroom experiences

Improving narrative writing through drama

Boys in the middle years of school (years 4, 5 and 6) in three suburban Sydney primary schools did not appear motivated by the learning experiences in their classrooms. Their teachers were concerned that they were not working at their level of ability because of this disengagement. A particular area identified through their year 3 writing assessment tasks was the writing of narrative. Initially the teachers worked together to benchmark the children's unassisted narratives and to develop detailed and relevant criteria for this stage.

Each classroom teacher worked with a mentor to use process-drama strategies[2] over a term with close study of the novel *The Iron Man* (Hughes 1968). Process drama (O'Neill 1995) uses a range of theatre strategies (such as sculpture, depiction or still image, hot-seating or questioning in role, playbuilding, mantle or enactment of the expert, readers' theatre) to enable participants to enact or walk in someone else's shoes (Ewing and Simons 2004) in a fictional situation. The imagined contexts allow students to suspend their real-world identities (Bolton 1984) to explore and make meanings considering other perspectives. This has been called finding *spaces* (Williams 1987) and *places* (Gleeson 2006) *to play* in multilayered texts. The emphasis is not on acting for an audience or on the performance itself: it is the educational process that is important. *The Iron Man* was chosen because the fable of a huge iron giant's sudden appearance in a farming community, the community members' initial reactions to his metal-eating tendencies and his later help in saving the world has many relevant themes. The text provoked real interest and many opportunities for student discussion.

Understandings about individual characters, particularly the Iron Man and the boy, Hugo, were developed through sculpting and later hot-seating. Students then wrote in role as the character they had embodied. The farmers' concerns about the Iron Man were debated before 'conscience alley', another process-drama strategy, was used to determine whether the Iron Man should be destroyed or allowed to continue to eat every piece of metal in sight. The children's selection of what they considered the most critical moments in the story led to animated discussion as they provided rationales for these choices. These critical moments were then expressed as still images (frozen moments/freeze-frames). Both sculpting and still images were recorded through digital cameras enabling ready access to the enactment experiences for reflection and subsequent writing activities. The use of the device 'mantle/enactment of the expert' was a culminating strategy to bring together students' learning through this text. Students took on roles as leaders of the great nations of the world. Having researched their chosen leader, they were 'experts' about what perspective this particular leader might take in a world threatened by a dangerous monster. Students in role as world leaders held a forum to discuss how the space-bat-angel-demon's demands could be met to avoid the destruction of the world. Solutions to this particular dilemma led to sophisticated philosophical discussions about achieving world peace.

Teachers involved across the three schools reported real changes in the students' attitude to learning. Boys who had previously been disengaged and unwilling to get involved in collaborative activities became enthusiastic participants in the learning activities, and this was reflected in the quality of their work, particularly through their oral discussion, participation in collaborative activities and writing. The drama activities built the students' vocabulary, understanding of syntax and metacognitive skills and this was evident in their subsequent narrative writing. Characters were described more richly, settings were portrayed in more detail and critical events in the plot were more contextualised when comparisons were made with earlier writing. Students explored the structure of the story, the author's point of view and how and why the text had been designed and constructed in a particular way.

Teaching Imaginatively

Funded by the Australian Literacy Educators Association (ALEA), seven primary teachers across the K–6 continuum in one Sydney school engaged in a project immersing children in Arts-based learning activities. They wanted to explore what teaching literacy creatively looked like at different stages of the K–6 primary curriculum (Ewing and Gibson 2007). While authentic children's literature to teach literacy was a major focus, each unit that was developed demonstrated meaningful integration across a number of key learning areas.

Research questions discussed in their action learning meetings (Revans 1983; Aubusson, Ewing and Hoban 2009) included:

- How do teachers know which books are authentic and worthwhile for classroom study?
- How do we help students to respond to what they read?
- Why is it important that we as teachers of primary children listen to and process the responses of our students to what they are reading?
- How do we encourage and foster a love of reading and narrative?

The teachers involved, Warhurst, Crawford, Ireland, Neale, Pickering, Rathmell and Watson (2008: 2-3), wrote: 'We wanted to make a difference so we spent time deciding what we think is important when teaching students to be critically literate … We wanted to show how art and drama can bring texts to life.' Initially they identified what criteria could be used to determine quality literary texts, made decisions about which texts were most appropriate for their students, and met regularly to discuss activities using imaginative Arts strategies they could incorporate into their units to encourage their students to respond creatively to texts. Examples of the students' talking, listening, reading and writing were benchmarked before the project began. Teachers compared these with students' work at various points along the way and recorded evidence of oral presentations, brainstorming, group discussions, drama and dance using digital cameras and electronic whiteboards to demonstrate increased student motivation and engagement, expanded vocabularies, increased use of imagery, and improved ability to listen and dialogue with each other. Students' writing demonstrated improved structural features as well as more sophisticated use of description and characterisation. Some specific classroom experiences are described below.

The kindergarten teacher Karen Crawford began her unit with *Lucy's Cat and the Rainbow Birds* (Hill and Tanner 2007). After a shared reading, the students mimed the story using percussion instruments to assist with representing the verbs (pouncing, crouching, gliding, slinking). They studied the use of alliteration (slinking, softly, stealthily, silently) to see what effect it had on the cat's actions in trying to catch the rainbow birds. The five-year-olds' initial benchmarked writing was characterised by very basic initial sentence structures (e.g., *My monster is purple*). This soon developed into more sophisticated texts (*Dear Monster, are you going to have a bath?*; *My monster likes to play Cluedo with me*; *My monster likes to eat strawberries and he is a little bit mean. He is nice to good people and horrible to bad people*). Crawford attributed the development of her students' writing to her blending of speech, music and drama with children's writing: 'Previously my passion for Speech and Drama wasn't associated with the literacy content of my teaching program … Blending through the project has made for a more rounded approach' (Warhurst *et al.* 2008: 4).

Year 3 teacher, Doug Neale, chose three of Tan's picture books: *The Red Tree* (2003), *The Lost Thing* (2001) and *The Arrival* (2007). As a benchmark, after a shared reading of *The Red Tree* the children wrote a response, then chose a line from the book and illustrated it. The students prepared questions for the girl in the story and hot-seated a class member in role. Their questions included: *Why was the red leaf always beside you?*; *Why do you feel sad?* Later the song 'Fragile' (Sting) was played and students used the lyrics to develop different and elaborated understandings of Tan's images. This in turn enabled a more complex reading of the images in *The Arrival*. Finally, the students jointly constructed a readers' theatre to tell a story they had created based on the *The Arrival*. Neale (Warhurst *et al.* 2008: 5) commented that their script showed 'an interesting interpretation of some of the characters and their role in the migrant's journey'.

Without exception the participant teachers reported that the project gave them a renewed energy about their teaching. They felt more confident about developing students' literacy outcomes. One teacher reflected:

> I have gone from using simple comprehension worksheets with disconnected texts of varying quality, to using carefully selected, quality texts and stimulating understanding through drama, art, writing, basic movie making, questioning and a multitude of other strategies … (Warhurst *et al.* 2008: 13).

Teachers believed that the students' improved responses were 'impressive', with the drama, art, movement, oral and written activities all providing a record of the students' achievements. The project leader Jan Warhurst writes about her year 3/4 students' response to her unit on *Blueback* (Winton 1997):

> The most powerful activity in terms of student engagement with the book was their improvised marine animals. They had extensively researched and told stories about them through drama and movement and we set them to the music of *Deep Sea Dreaming* (Elena-Katz Chernin). Students then wrote narratives which included descriptions of where the creatures of the sea were located … Our class mural grew out of the students' fascination of images and themes in the story. Drawings by groups of two, three or four students reflected their own interpretations of the story and these were translated into a paneled mural using batik, tie dye and appliquéd techniques (Warhurst *et al.* 2008: 9).

One of Warhurst's students provided a final response to close study of *Blueback* through the following poem:

> Under the Sea
> Wise round eyes,
> A pot-bellied figure
> Gracefully gliding along,

Joyfully nosing through the clear aqua liquid
No nonentity was he.
Thick rubber lips, like waterlogged cotton
Sucking in the crustaceans past by,
Small silver fish, pass on their messages,
Watch out for the Groper nearby!

Crystal pink coral sways gently in the current,
Bowing to the king of the sea,
And as he swims past,
With a wink and a twirl,
He nudges it appreciatively.

The Catfish and the seahorses,
All swim out of his way,
As he passes through the crevice,
With a soothing, gentle sway.

The Sun dipped down the horizon,
It was as quiet as a mouse.
And the old Blue Groper slept soundlessly,
In his comfy, brown rock-house.

Similarly the year 5/6 teacher Jenny Pickering developed a unit based on the novel *Hana's Suitcase* (Levine 2003) and the picture book *Rose Blanche* (Innocenti 1985). The students used tableau to convey their understanding of the holocaust and the themes addressed in both texts including identity, resistance and survival. Hot-seating or questioning in role enabled them to clarify what happened to the characters in the stories, and this led to writing in role as Hana. In recording their feelings about Hana, the students developed both a voice collage and visual images. Teacher-in-role and sculpting were used to explore Rose Blanche's loss of innocence when she found the Jewish children in the concentration camp. The transformation of the writing of one of Pickering's student case studies, 'Jason', follows. His initial response benchmark (March 2008) to Burningham's *Come Away from the Water Shirley* (2003) is followed by writing in role as Hana several weeks later. The final example is his response to *Rose Blanche* which concluded the unit.

Writing sample 1

Today we read a book called 'Come Away from the Water Shirley' by John Birmingham. In the story a girl goes to the beach one day but she is really bored so she thinks of something to do. After a while she starts imagining herself on a boat with a dog she sees running along the beach. But in real life she is bored.

I did not really like this book because it did not make sense to me.

Writing sample 2

Winter 1939

Dear Jason

I'm having the worst time of my life. Some warriors called Nazis aren't letting us do anything. I'm not allowed to play with my friends or play in the playground. I wish I could come and live with you in Australia. I'm so sad and I'm really devastated!

Yesterday George and me made a time capsule. We expressed our feelings by putting down all the things we really hated about the Nazis and we wrote down all the things we miss doing like playing with our friends and going to the movies. Ooh, that reminds me, me and George went to the movies to see 'Snow White and the 7 Dwarves' and just when we were about to go in there was a sign, 'No Jews Allowed'. I was so angry I felt like screaming so loud that everybody could hear me …

Writing Sample 3

Rose Blanche is a fantastic, sad, interesting book written by Roberto Innocenti. It is about a girl called Rose Blanche who lives in Germany in world war two. Rose finds a strange place called a concentration camp full of sick people. She decides to visit them every day and give them food.

I think the characters are very exciting and represent a lot of things like …
Rose represents innocence just like Hanna Brady.
Rose also represents the people who were against the war.
The fat mayor represents greed.
The fat mayors red swashtica band represents himself on Hittlers and the Nazis side.

This book to me is about greed, war and innocence. This story relates to Hannas suitcase so much. The books are about two innocent little girls who are unfortunately caught up in world war two. Fortunately Rose is fiction unfortunately Hanna Brady is not. Unfortunately at the end of both stories both girls died. I find world war two the most interesting part of history and I would love to learn more.

Conclusion

Both of the above projects have addressed the embedding of the Arts in the literacy curriculum itself, developed the teachers' professional knowledge, and encouraged artistic pedagogy in their classroom practice. Each project also emphasises teacher ownership of the professional learning processes through action learning. The action-learning cycle includes time for teacher analysis of the issues, planning of the initiative, and discussion, analysis and reflection after the implementation stage. Reflection may be through professional conversations, journals, portfolios, exhibits or performances. In each project teachers discussed the way students were able to use process drama, dance and visual art as a starting point to enhance critical literacy outcomes. The focus on enactment or embodiment provided a trigger to encourage students to begin to value multiple meanings in quality texts and to understand and respect perspectives different from their own, subsequently reflected in their discussion and writing.

'Literacy education' and its predecessor 'reading and writing instruction' are arenas of constant heated contestation among educators, the media and communities more broadly. The educational place and distinctive contribution of the Arts and their relationship to other curriculum areas are also much debated and often undervalued, despite the growing unequivocal research evidence demonstrating their centrality to all learning and to the development of creativity. Educators have an enormous responsibility to teach literacy imaginatively through the Arts. In Mary Beattie's words:

> As individuals gain new understandings of how the different forms of thinking they have experienced through the Arts have allowed them to create different forms of meaning, they have also begun to appreciate the distinctive ways the arts have enabled them to think, feel, see and imagine new ways of knowing and being (2009: 3).

References

Abbs, P. (1987) *Living Powers: The Arts in Education*. London: Falmer.

Apple, M. (1990) *Ideology and Curriculum*, 2nd edn. London: Routledge.

Aubusson, P., Ewing, R. and Hoban, G. (2009) *Action Learning in Primary Schools: Rethinking Professional Development*. London: Routledge.

Baldwin, P. and Fleming, K. (2003) *Teaching Literacy through Drama: Creative Approaches*. London: Routledge Falmer.

Bamford, A. (2006) *The Wow Factor: Global Research Compendium of the Impact of Arts Education*. New York: Waxmann.

Beattie, M. (2009) *The Quest for Meaning: Teaching, Learning and the Arts*. Rotterdam: Sense Publishers.

Bolton, G. (1984) *Drama as Education*. London: Longman.

Bruner, J. (1986) *Actual Minds, Possible Worlds*. Cambridge, MA: Harvard University Press.

Burningham, J. (2003) *Come Away from the Water, Shirley*. Random House: London.

Catterall, J., Chapleau, R. and Iwanga, J. (1999) Involvement in the arts and human development. In E. Fiske (ed.) *Champions of Change: The Impact of the Arts on Learning*. Washington, DC: The Arts Partnership.

Crumpler, T. and Schneider, J. (2002) Writing with their whole being: a cross study analysis of children's writing from five classrooms using process drama. *Research in Drama Education* 7 (1): 61-79.

Damasio, A. (1994) *Descartes Error: Emotion, Reason and the Human Brain*. New York: Avon Books.

Deasy, R. (ed.) (2002) *Critical Links: Learning in the Arts and Student Academic and Social Development*. Washington, DC: Arts Education Partnership.

Dewey, J. (1989) Art as experience. In J. Boydston (ed.) *John Dewey: The Later Works, 1925–1953*, X. Carbondale: Southern Illinois University Press.

Egan,K. (1988) *Primary Understanding*. New York: Routledge.

Egan, K. (1992) *Imagination in Teaching and Learning: Ages 8–15*. London: Routledge.

Egan, K. (2007) *A Brief Guide to Imaginative Education. Imagination in Education Research Group* (IERG). http://www.ierg.net (accessed 22 June 2009).

Eisner, E. (2002) *The Arts and the Creation of Mind*. New Haven: Yale University Press.

Eisner, E. (2005) Opening a shuttered window. An introduction to a special section on the arts and the intellect. *Phi Delta Kappan*, September: 8-10.

Ewing, R. and Gibson, R. (2007) Creative teaching or teaching creatively? Using creative arts strategies in preservice teacher education. *Waikato Journal of Education* (Special issue on Creative Research in the Arts) 13: 159-78.

Ewing, R. and Simons, J. (2004) *Beyond the Script: Take 2*. Sydney: Primary English Teaching Association.

Ewing, R., Miller, C. and Saxton, J. (2008) Drama and contemporary picture books in the middle years. In J. Hughes, M. Anderson and J. Manuel (eds.) *Drama Teaching in English: Imagination, Action and Engagement*. Melbourne: Oxford University Press, 121-35.

Fiske, E. (1999) *Champions of Change: The Impact of Arts on Learning*. Washington, DC: Arts Education Partnership/Presidents' Committee on the Arts and Humanities.

Freeman, W. (1995) *Societies of Brains: A Study in the Neuroscience of Love and Hate*. Hillsdale, NJ: Lawrence Erlbaum.

Freire, P. (1985) *The Politics of Education: Culture, Power and Liberation*. New York: Bergin & Garvey.

Freire, P. (1986) *Pedagogy of the Oppressed*. Harmondsworth: Penguin.

Gire, K. (1996) *Windows of the Soul*. Grand Rapids, MI: Zondervan Publishing House.

Gleeson, L. (2006) Places to play: stories as an adventure playground. Paper presented at The National Conference on Future Directions in Literacy, University of Sydney, NSW, Australia, 3 March 2006.

Greene, M. (1995) *Releasing the Imagination: Essays on Education, the Arts and Social Change*. San Francisco: Jossey Bass.

Heath, S.B. (2000) Seeing our way into learning. *Cambridge Journal of Education* 30 (1): 121-31.

Heathcote, D. and Bolton, G. (1995) *Drama for Learning*. Portsmouth: Heinemann.

Hill, A. and Tanner, J. (2007) *Lucy's Cat and the Rainbow Birds*. Melbourne: Penguin.

Hoffman Davis, J. (2005) Redefining Ratso Rizzo: learning from the arts about process and reflection. *Phi Delta Kappan*, September: 11-17.

Hughes, T. (1968) *The Iron Man*. London: Faber & Faber.

Innocenti, R. (1985). *Rose Blanche*. London: Jonathan Cape.

Keifer, B. (1995) *The Potential of Picture Books: From Visual Literacy to Aesthetic Understanding*. Englewood Cliffs, NJ: Prentice Hall.

Levine, K. (2003) *Hana's Suitcase*. Morton Grove, IL: Albert Whitman.

Lowenfeld, V. (1947) *Creative and Mental Growth*. New York: Macmillan.

McNaughton, M. (1997) Drama and children's writing: a study of the influence of drama on the imaginative writing of primary school children. *Research in Drama Education* 2 (1): 55-86.

Miller, C. and Saxton, J. (2004) *Into the Story: Language in Action through Drama*. Portsmouth, NH: Heinemann.

Mills, K. (2008) Will large-scale assessments raise literacy standards in Australian schools? *Australian Journal of Language and Literacy* 31 (3): 211-26.

O'Neill, C. (1995) *Dramaworlds: A Framework for Process Drama.* Portsmouth, NH: Heinemann.

O'Toole, J. (2008) The arts and creativity: a manifesto for school. In C. Sinclair, N. Jeanneret and J. O'Toole (eds.) *Education in the Arts.* Melbourne: Oxford University Press, xxiii-xxvii.

O'Toole, J. and Dunn, J. (2002) *Pretending to Learn.* Frenchs Forest: Pearson Education Australia.

Piaget, J. (1962) *Play, Dreams and Imitation in Childhood.* London: Routledge & Kegan Paul.

Read, H. (1964) *Art and Education.* Melbourne: Cheshire.

Revans, R. (1983) *ABC of Action Learning.* Southall: Chartwell-Bratt.

Robinson, K. (1999) *All our Futures: Creativity, Culture and Education.* Report to the National Advisory Committee on Creative and Cultural Education. London.

Schellenberg, G. and Peretz, I. (2008) Music, language and cognition. Unresolved issues. *Trends in Cognitive Sciences* 12: 45-46.

Shor, I. (1987) *A Pedagogy for Liberation.* Westport, CT: Greenwood.

Siegesmund, R. (2005) Teaching qualitative reasoning. *Phi Delta Kappan,* September: 18-23.

Slade, P. (1954) *Child Drama.* London: Cassell.

Strauss, S., Goodman, K. and Paulson, E. (2009) Brain research and reading: how emerging concepts in neuroscience support a meaning construction view of the reading process. *Educational Research and Review* 4 (2): 21-33.

Tan, S. (2001) *The Lost Thing.* Melbourne: Lothian.

Tan, S.(2003) *The Red Tree.* Melbourne: Simply Read Books.

Tan, S. (2007) *The Arrival.* Sydney: Hodder.

Tan, S. (2008) Interview with Margaret Throsby, Radio National. Australian Broadcasting Commission, 12 June.

Vygotsky, L. (1971) *The Psychology of Art.* Boston: MIT Press.

Warhurst, J., Crawford, K., Ireland, J., Neale, D., Pickering, J., Rathmell, C. and Watson, G. (2008) Improving literacy pedagogy and outcomes through the creative arts. Paper presented at Australian Literacy Educators Conference, Adelaide, July.

Williams, G. (1987) Spaces to play: the use of analyses of narrative structure in classroom work with children's literature. In M. Saxby and G. Winch (eds.) *Give them Wings: The Experience of Children's Literature.* Melbourne: Macmillan.

Williams, L. and Gordon, E. (2007) Dynamic organization of the emotional brain: responsivity, stability and instability. *The Neuroscientist* 13: 349-70.

Winton, T. (1997) *Blueback.* Chippendale, NSW: Picador.

Notes

[1] **Robyn Ewing** is Professor of Teacher Education and the Arts at the University of Sydney's Faculty of Education and Social Work. Formerly a primary teacher, she has lectured, researched and published in curriculum, English, drama and teacher education for more than 20 years. Her recent publications include: with Susan Groundwater-Smith and Rosie Le Cornu, *Teaching: Challenges and Dilemmas* (Melbourne: Cengage, 2010); with Jennifer

Simons, *Beyond the Script Take 2: Drama in the Classroom* (Sydney: Primary English Teaching Association, 2004); *Curriculum and Assessment: A Narrative Approach* (Melbourne: Oxford University Press, 2009); with Peter Aubusson and Garry Hoban, *Action Learning: Reframing Teachers' Professional Learning and Development* (London: Routledge, 2009); (ed.), *Beyond the Reading Wars: Towards a Balanced Approach to Helping Children Learn to Read* (Sydney: Primary English Teaching Association, 2006); and with Tom Lowrie and Joy Higgs (eds.), *Teaching and Communicating: Rethinking Professional Experiences* (Melbourne: Oxford University Press, 2009).

[2] For details about specific drama strategies mentioned in the chapter see, for example, Baldwin and Fleming 2003; Ewing and Simons 2004; Miller and Saxton 2004; or O'Toole and Dunn 2002.

6   The social context of literacy acquisition: achieving good beginnings

Tony Vinson[1]

Introduction

My exploration of what is needed to give all of Australia's children a good start to their education has taken me to the springs of social disadvantage, a life condition affecting the individuals, families and communities with whom I have worked throughout my five decades of social-work practice. My conclusion is that, in the absence of compensatory educational experiences and appropriate forms of social support, a substantial number of today's socially disadvantaged small children are positioned to become tomorrow's frustrated and rejected adults. I want to begin by recalling some scenes that I have encountered during my recent observations of 20 of New South Wales' pre-schools attached to public schools and/or kindergartens in public schools. The study was conducted in 2005–2006, and the findings were reported to a body called the Public Education Alliance at a conference staged at State Parliament House, Sydney, and received wide media coverage. I must emphasise that, by design, the majority of the schools in my sample were located in not-well-off communities in the Australian state of New South Wales, and in some instances they served decidedly disadvantaged neighbourhoods, including some Aboriginal ones. The scenes that I recount are fundamental reality tests for measures intended to provide all of our children with good beginnings to their education. Moreover, though they are drawn from Australian observation, they are relevant for all other societies where young children experience social disadvantage.

Some scenes from our schools

- One four year-old boy arrived at school possessing a vocabulary of two words – 'bad boy'.
- At one country school I found some four-year-olds confused about their gender identity. They didn't know what to do when they heard

'Boys go here, girls go there'. At a Sydney school serving a disadvantaged area a similar problem was evidenced when girls were asked to stand up and they looked blankly at the teacher and asked, 'Am I a girl?'

- At another school a child whose speech was almost unintelligible became so frustrated that he hit himself while trying to communicate.
- One pre-school teacher in Western Sydney said, 'When I place a pen, a paintbrush, a book in some children's hands all I get is a quizzical look as if to say "What is this? What do I do with it?" Some of the four-year-olds here can't form intelligible sounds. They need a lot of individualised help to hear and say words. Their parents have very limited language and can't help them much. Professional speech help would be good but in reality, it falls on the shoulders of the teachers. To start to help these children at five is too late – two would be good.'
- A teacher at another Sydney school said, 'It makes learning a word more difficult if you have no experience or knowledge of what it denotes. Some of our children have never left their suburb, let alone taken the train to the city. Their news is predictable – "I went to the shops".' This theme was elaborated upon at another school where teachers said that the children lacked any phonic awareness. 'Many of our children are not encouraged to speak. What is said to them is largely directive. What they utter consists largely of nouns and labels with few connecting words. There has been an absence of conversation in their lives; they have not seen a book and have no idea that it conveys meaning.' At this point another teacher commented: 'That's why we put such an emphasis on excursions. From the bus windows the four- and five-year-olds see things for the first time – the airport, the harbour bridge, tall buildings. As they go through Sydney they are in awe, in shock. Their wide-eyed expressions and open mouths tell you all you need to know about their reactions.' At another school the principal said much the same thing: 'We take them on excursions to extend their knowledge of the world'.
- At a number of Sydney suburban primary schools it is frequently the case that a child arrives possessing three or four words. One principal commented, 'We refer the parents and their child to a regional health centre but an eighteen months delay in providing treatment is common'. The principal added, 'We don't set out to be social workers but if we don't attend to the children's social needs little or no learning is going to take place. It is better that this occurs at four years of age rather than five.'
- Sometimes siblings of the children observed displayed the same

speech difficulties. The associated delays in phonic ability block reading development. In some extreme cases my attention was drawn to a form of selective mutism connected with school anxiety. There were also some speech impediments, resulting in little interaction with teachers. In these cases the teachers were thrown back on their own resources in trying to overcome the problem in pre-school and they modelled the enunciation of sounds that the children had not heard spoken correctly – vowels and 'h' sounds, medial sounds, pronouncing 'g' at the end of words, and the like. Success in these endeavours often required imaginative ways of gaining parental and community participation, for example, using itinerant community readers, or bridging school and home by using multilingual teachers. In one instance, the streets of a country town were closed while people celebrated the presence of a leather-clad *bikie* book devotee adorned with a sign 'born to read' in place of the more usual 'born to ride'.

- At another school a teacher commented, 'Coming from stressful backgrounds our children are continually worried … The children are totally lacking in confidence, so much so that they can't take the kind of risks involved in learning. Asked to take a number of toys out of a box they withdraw from the task and hide their face in their hands.'
- Children's non-exposure to books deprives them of the enchantment that can follow when that encounter happens in an exciting way. One child I observed recently experienced the opening of a larger-than-life book as something akin to the opening of a magic door. He touched the book and gazed at it in wonder.
- A requirement of effective learning is having the energy to participate. During my visits I met some children visibly lacking in energy – lying on a table, sitting half asleep, slumped in a corner. These children responded well to a simple mid-morning breakfast and, according to their teachers, it was possibly the only meal some of them would have that day.

The surest sign of whether our nation has a soul is whether it cherishes *all* of its children. Possession of a rising domestic product, the finest military hardware and millionaires to spare tell only of other priorities unconnected to our most human values. Unless there is a serious commitment to upholding every child's birthright to acquire the educational and personal foundations for a full and satisfying life, we fail the first test of any civilised community. That involves doing justice by the most vulnerable among us, our children, and especially socially disadvantaged children.

My earlier examples illustrate how some children miss out on what has been referred to as the phase of *emergent literacy*, during which they do not read and write in conventional ways, but can come to understand many features and functions of the spoken and printed word, all relevant to eventual entry to literacy (Smith and Dickinson 2002). Children who have never held a pencil or a book have few opportunities to rehearse the conventions of print, the structure of texts, letter recognition or to achieve phonological awareness. Moreover, young children with little experience of conversation will find it difficult to acquire the use of decontextualised oral language (Dickinson and Tabors 2001), of the kind that is essential for participation in school talk. Failure to overcome this initial deficiency can have major flow-on consequences for a child's education and life prospects. Considerations of social justice, therefore, require two things to occur, each of which is examined below:

1. the school system must employ the substantial body of relevant knowledge available to narrow the gap between children coming from educationally and socially disadvantaged backgrounds and children more favourably placed in these respects; and
2. social policy and social provision must support these endeavours.

Above I have outlined the broad context in which the current provision of prior-to-school care and education needs to be considered. Expressions of respect for the preciousness of our children and the practical priorities that should flow from that commitment are sometimes declaratory rather than implemented. That this can happen is a tribute to our society's ability to block out discomforting facts. Those who have taken off the 'blinkers' talk of the *school to prison pipeline* to describe the concentrated flow of youth from some disadvantaged neighbourhoods to punishment institutions. There have been repeated assertions by education administrators and state officials in America that early reading test scores are used to help predict future prison accommodation needs.

Some research evidence for the importance of early childhood educational intervention

Significant research evidence from several sources points to the need for intervention in the welfare of very young disadvantaged children, using positive and helpful means to transform their lives, thereby avoiding bleak and unsatisfying futures. As Victor Hugo says in *Les Misérables*, if the soul is left in darkness, sins will be committed: the guilty ones are not those who commit the sin, but those who cause the darkness. In secular terms, what constitutes 'light' in the pre-school lives of our children? What emerges from all the best recent research evidence is the fundamental importance of early learning. The common ground in the available research is the importance of children's readiness to learn in their earliest years. If this readiness is not exploited and fully used, serious negative consequences will follow. Other more refined analyses will follow but an article in *Business Week* (2002) put it baldly:

> Children form basic cognitive abilities in their earliest years and those who don't get exposed to letters, numbers and social skills at home quickly lag behind those who do … That's why we have to get 'em while they're still tots (Starr 2002: 16).

Of course, as early education teachers are only too well aware, the situation is more complicated than simple exposure to 'letters, numbers and social skills', important though they are. Considerable debate often emerges in the teaching profession about the rival merits of different literacy pedagogies, though it seems clear that emergence of some early understanding of literacy represents a foundation on which teachers can build skilled, specific instruction to help children to become 'fluent processors of written language' (Smith and Dickinson 2002). However, this chapter does not seek to engage directly with the debates over rival literacy pedagogies. That is because the primary concern of this chapter is with the necessity of taking account of the educationally and socially deprived backgrounds of significant numbers of children in providing and structuring early education. It is a concern recently stated in explicit terms by six British Columbia university research groups that have found:

> School-level literacy risk is systematically related to contextual factors: high risk schools tend to be characterised by the greatest developmental and socioeconomic vulnerability … from school to school, intervention models must vary as a function of the school population and characteristics (Human Early Learning Partnership 2006: 1).

A recent RAND Corporation overview of *Early Childhood Interventions* in America (Karoly, Kilburn and Cannon 2005: xvi) included a large-scale longitudinal study indicating that disadvantaged children not only arrive at school less well prepared than the relatively advantaged, but that early gaps persist and even widen as children progress through school. The children in question more frequently drop out of high school, and have more unemployment, welfare dependency, delinquency and crime rates. The RAND review concluded, 'Even if only a portion of these detrimental outcomes in childhood and adulthood can be averted, the benefits may be substantial' (Karoly, Kilburn and Cannon 2005: xvi). More generally, the RAND assessment identified 20 studies of early childhood intervention projects that had employed scientifically rigorous methods of evaluation. Statistically significant benefits were found in at least two-thirds of the programmes reviewed. The magnitudes of the favourable effects were sometimes sizable and long lasting, particularly with respect to educational progress, labour market outcomes, welfare dependency and pro-social behaviours, as illustrated by the High Scope studies mentioned below. The estimates of returns to society for each dollar invested extended from over $1 to more than $17. The available evidence indicates that the economic returns from investing in early intervention programmes are larger when higher-risk populations are targeted but that universal programmes can yield benefits two and a half times the cost.

Some of the demonstrable benefits of high-quality pre-school programmes increase in magnitude as longitudinal studies are extended over increasing periods of time. A good example is the High Scope Perry Preschool study conducted in America (ECCD Briefs 1999: 1). Three- and four-year-olds were randomly allocated to a group receiving a high-quality pre-school programme and a control group. By the age of 27, only one-fifth as many programme group members as members of the no-programme group had had multiple arrests and only one-third as many were ever arrested for drug dealing. The earnings and general economic status and educational attainments of the programme group were significantly higher, and their relationships were more stable. The researchers have calculated a sevenfold benefits:cost ratio of the programme investment returned to the public – a better investment than the stock market during the same period. A similar picture emerged for subjects who had reached 40 years of age (Schweinhart *et al.* 2005).

The policy-oriented American National Institute for Early Education Research has found that children living in poverty are 18 months behind the average child when they start kindergarten (Barnett, Brown and Shore: 2004). The same Institute has charted the degree of school readiness of children against their family incomes and the gradient is steep and continuous (see figure 1).

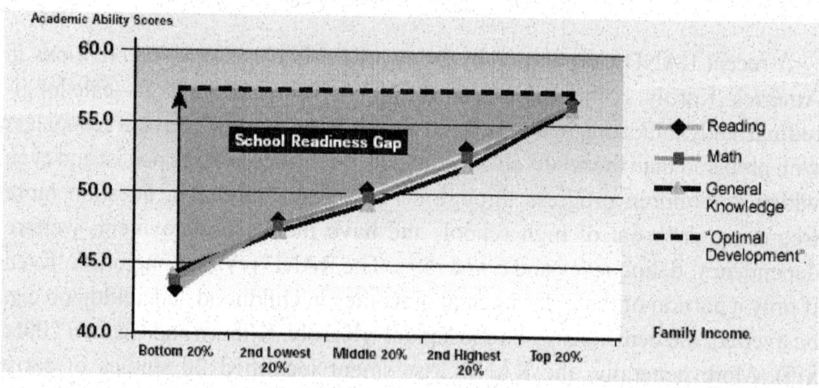

Figure 1. Academic abilities of entering kindergarteners by family income
(Source: American National Institute for Early Education Research)

In the Australian context, there are uncertainties in some instances about which prior-to-school arrangements involve pre-schooling as distinct from childcare. Nevertheless, a similar gradient is apparent in the Australian Bureau of Statistics pre-school participation rates for four-year-old children of varying household incomes (Australian Bureau of Statistics 2004). Children's pre-school participation tends to increase in line with household income, ranging from 49% of four-year-olds in households in the lowest income quintile to 66% of those from households in the highest income quintile.

The first required response: the school system and narrowing the gap

Assuming for the moment ways of engaging their participation, how can educational and care services be established that significantly improve the early education, literacy acquisition and life prospects of disadvantaged children? One starting point in answering this question is to consider whether the best insights of international practice are understood and distilled into curriculum documents. In the Australian context, for example, curriculum statements identify play as the major medium of learning in early childhood, and they emphasise the notion of the child as citizen with a right to be respected as a full human being (see, for example, NSW Department of Community Services 2002: 15-18). Relationships in children's services are seen as existing to promote the well-being of the child, including the growth of a positive self-identity and enjoyment of and learning from relationships. The pre-schools that I observed in my study employ these relationship principles in their day-to-day work.

What is the kernel of these views and the research and experience upon which they are based? First, childhood education and care are inseparable. Children's needs are interwoven: intellectual growth and the need for play and friendship, and social, physical and emotional development are all interconnected. This theme is of central importance to an important discussion paper prepared by Uniting Care Burnside, SDN Children's Services (formerly the Sydney Day Nursery) and Uniting Care Children's Services (2005). It is not only disadvantaged children who benefit from early childhood education and care services, but measures such as reduced class sizes are especially beneficial for children experiencing developmental difficulties, as well as those who are socio-economically disadvantaged (Lynch 2004).

Second, more is involved in narrowing the gap than simply ensuring the adoption of pre-school education programmes, or moving forward to an earlier age the beginning of school instruction. Since the 1980s, leading early childhood practitioners have argued for adoption of different pedagogies, and they have, for example, expressed concern about the wisdom of excessively didactic, formal instructional practices for young children (Elkind 1986: 631-36). Contemporary research (Marcon 2002) confirms that these early concerns were warranted. Pushing children too soon may actually backfire. The foundation of critical thinking may be found in early childhood experiences that foster curiosity, initiative, independence and effective choice. Moreover, it is important that teachers ensure an appropriate readiness to learn in the young children in their care. They are also assisted by provision of effective links to other supportive services, though these are not always as effective as they could be because of lack of adequate staff. I shall say a little about each of these matters.

Readiness

How do the desirable characteristics alluded to above match up with the approach to early schooling that I have observed? Without exception, the attached pre-schools emphasised children's need to acquire those social skills and attributes of self-sufficiency that are needed to participate in the more formal learning that follows in kindergarten and later years. Learning to sit safely, give attention, feel comfortable with non-family adults and children, operate in a group, take turns, socialise, sit with others at a table, respect and not interfere with the well-being of others, take directions, begin to be self-sufficient in small ways (like packing and unpacking their bag and choosing between their 'little and big meal'), become accustomed to routine and gradually acquire, or have reinforced, rudimentary principles of considerate conduct – these are invariant features of the pre-schools that I observed.

Accompanying these strands of social progress is careful assessment of the overall development of each child, usually employing formal professional tools and frameworks, and identifying specific abilities that need to be exercised and strengthened – such as fine motor skills and use of receptive and expressive language. This is where the varied impediments to development and learning which I included in the illustrative scenes from our schools above enter the picture. This is also where early education teachers can be seen drawing heavily upon their professional learning in making fine judgements about what needs to be done to assist children with special needs. As one pre-school teacher put it, 'We draw upon every bit of the academic knowledge that we covered in our tertiary studies'. The teachers apply such knowledge while working barefooted in the sand pit, at the planning board carefully devising the pre-school programme, and interviewing carers in the privacy of their office. 'Readying' in this context means both seizing the opportunity afforded by the pre-school year to overcome problems in children before they are further consolidated and undermine later learning, and preparing the children for the more formal teaching and learning that lie ahead.

There is one catch: frequently the requisite specialised back-up services to support teachers are not available at opportune times, and so resourceful teachers set about acquiring additional skills in an attempt to give every child a good beginning. Children's language problems loom large in this picture, and I will shortly say more about that issue.

As the year progresses, readying the children for kindergarten involves greater involvement with the rest of the school. Participation in celebratory occasions (Easter hat, and book character parades, and the like), some assemblies, visits to kindergarten classrooms, familiarisation with kindergarten teachers (including the latter's rostered playground duties), the transmission of children's work and progress that is made available to the teachers who follow and to parents/caregivers, and teacher-to-teacher discussions are among the devices used. This integration of pre-school and kindergarten within the public schools is of immense importance in the care and development of children of disadvantaged backgrounds. Similar exchanges can occur to some degree when the pre-school is detached from the public school via means like Transition Programs and Primary Connect. Cooperative practices are especially evident between community-based pre-schools that are established and operated by non-profit local associations and public schools, especially in country areas. By year's end, a child's recognition of colours, some ability to count and apply numbers to things and do so on a small scale but in a fluent way, to recognise her or his name and begin to write it, to sound some letters, the capacity to handle and use the tools of learning – a brush, a pen, a book, scissors, a 'mouse' (in relation to a child's special computer) – these were among the precursor educational goals in the pre-schools observed.

To claim that the system I have described is effective in providing 'significant benefits' for disadvantaged children is not to claim magical powers for them of completely overriding the consequences of disadvantage. More subtle recent evaluations of the impact of programmes intended to better prepare disadvantaged children for school have emphasised the major educational contribution of informal influences on learning. One study even found that the largest advance in some young children's educational performance occurred during an annual holiday period (Entwisle, Alexander and Olson 2005: 1458-1502). The enriching experiences available to some (more advantaged) children during summer holiday periods can see their rate of learning peak during such times.

This means that the gap between advantaged and disadvantaged children is extremely difficult to close, but the gap can be significantly narrowed. However, that result is not produced by good intentions alone. High-quality early childhood care and education services employ staff who are educated for their work, have decent working conditions, work with groups of children of manageable size and provide activities that match the principles of the previously described curriculum framework and similar international documents. That is to say, they require the provision of challenging but non-didactic, creative, enjoyable activities for children that ensure consistent adult and peer groups in stable social and physical environments (Friendly and Lero 2002).

Links to other services, agencies

All countries no doubt establish supportive links between schools and various agencies that exist to serve social welfare. This discussion again draws on Australian experience, and there will be parallels elsewhere. There are variations in the linkages between pre-schools and other service providers in Australia. Typically the support network includes a regional health centre, a local hospital, a non-government family or children's service, and specialist district education officials of the Department of Education and Training. Almost all pre-schools make referrals to regional health centres but complain of long delays, particularly in accessing speech therapy. In the course of my study, there were repeated claims of delays of 18 months in obtaining services. In almost all of the schools visited parents lacked the funds needed to gain private services for their children. Some schools regarded the problem as being so severe that they supplemented funds from other sources with scarce operating funds, believing that to not do so would undermine all of the other professional efforts to help the children. One school, tired of launching children burdened with a speech problem into formal schooling, devoted scarce funds to securing the services of a language specialist one day per week. However, the part-time appointee commented, 'I could not do justice to the children in this school with speech problems if I worked five days a week'. The area concerned is one of the most disadvantaged neighbourhoods in New South Wales. In a similarly ranked country area served by a community pre-school, after careful consideration it was concluded that 19 of 43 students needed the services of a speech therapist.

The picture that emerges overall from my study of a selection of public pre-schools and kindergartens suggests that the pre-school teachers made substantial use of their relevant background knowledge to narrow the gap between children coming from educationally and socially disadvantaged backgrounds and those more favourably placed in these respects. I found that the major shortcoming was the inadequate development of partnerships between the schools and social agencies intended to provide specialist support. Nowhere was this more evident than in the access made available to speech therapists to assist children with speech problems.

The second required response: supportive social policy and provision

Uniting Care Burnside and affiliate organisations are right to insist that education and care services should be universally available for all three- and four-year-olds and that more vulnerable or disadvantaged children should have access to such services at an even earlier age depending on their circumstances. Those goals are not unusual but mainstream policy in many countries. 'Starting Strong', an OECD (2001a) survey, found a surge of policy attention to early childhood education and care in OECD countries over the preceding decade. Most of the countries studied declared an aim to give all children at least two years of free publicly funded provision before beginning compulsory schooling.

Two countries whose early childcare and education programmes I have had the opportunity to study at first-hand provide services that contribute significantly to overcoming the social and educational disadvantage that I illustrated at the outset of this chapter. For more than three decades childcare has been a priority issue for public authorities in Sweden. Providing for the well-being of the young and the promotion of greater equality between the sexes have been driving forces. Reforms in the past few years have been promoted under national legislation and guided by the National Agency for Education (Skolverket 2005) but administered at the municipal level. Central government outlines the overall childcare objectives while the local authorities are responsible for implementing them. Today, the National Agency for School Improvement (2007) and the National Agency for Education are the central supervisory authorities for childcare and schooling. There is a modest ceiling for the amount parents are required to pay. The reforms have seen a national pre-school curriculum developed and assured the availability of childcare to all with fees so low that no child is excluded (ESTIA 2003). The pre- and compulsory school curriculums cohere so that an important part of the early curriculum relates to basic democratic values and solidarity. This is not mere tokenism. Visiting the town of Malmö I was surprised to come across a group of very young children bearing placards parading up and down a street. When I later contacted the school to express my interest in what was happening I was told that the children had decided to stage a demonstration against people driving fast past their school. They had informed the staff of their wish, and the teachers were obliged to support their protest.

Since 1997 the UK government has made an unprecedented effort to increase investment in families and young children (OECD 2001b). A national childcare strategy was announced in 1998 to be given practical effect by locally based Early Years Development and Childcare Partnerships operating collaboratively with the local education and social services authorities. Over 500 Sure Start local programmes have been opened since 1998 offering a range of early learning, health and family services to parents and children in the most disadvantaged areas (Schneider *et al.* 2007: 914). The aims of Sure Start are neatly encapsulated in this summary:

> To work with parents-to-be, parents and children to promote the physical, intellectual and social development of babies and young children – particularly those who are disadvantaged – so that they can flourish at home and when they get to school, thereby breaking the cycle of disadvantage for the current generation of young children.

Assuring the best possible beginning for socially disadvantaged children was, in the first instance, covered by the allocation of special funding for disadvantaged areas through the Sure Start initiative. Curriculum Guidelines for the Foundation Stage (3–5 years) bring coherence to teachers' endeavours without being overly prescriptive about content (OFSTED 2007). The task of a National Office for Standards in Education (OFSTED 2006) is to formulate national child service standards. Although reliant in ways similar to the Swedish policies upon local initiatives, the national strategy still sets measurable objectives.

Despite the 'mainstreaming' of Sure Start from 2005, the national investment in young children is still impressive. A beginning has been made in linking childcare to a wide range of services that support parents especially by way of health and social care through Sure Start centres and extended schools, which also boost the availability of childcare. Many schools are offering extended services, and there is evidence indicating that study support is having beneficial effects on the achievements of children and young people. Services are being developed after consultation with parents and the local community. Extended services will include support for parents, family learning opportunities and easy referral to specialist support services. The government's investment in early education and care has grown to the point where all three- and four-year-olds have available 15 hours of free education and care for 38 weeks in a year.

Most of the early programmes have now become Sure Start children's centres offering a one-stop shop of help, advice, childcare and early education for children under five and their families, including antenatal and postnatal services. Considerable emphasis is being placed on effective ways of communicating information about services to families that might otherwise miss out – for example, a free phone 'hot line' to a Children's Information Service. In fact, one of the themes most emphasised by Sure Start executives when I visited the programme in mid 2006 was the importance of engaging 'hard to reach' families, shown by the national evaluation to be one of the impediments to the success of the programme. In the light of the research, all Sure Start children's centres should:

- identify families that may be excluded, and tailor services to their needs;
- track patterns of engagement and use outreach and home visiting to invite the involvement of families who are unlikely to visit a centre;
- keep parents up-to-date with how their child is doing and encourage them to be actively involved;
- develop strong multi-agency partnerships, particularly with health services.

After years of talk about learning from these precedents, Australia is finally taking practical steps to guarantee that our pre-schoolers benefit from early education programmes. The Australian government is committed to ensuring that all children in the year before formal schooling will have access to quality early childhood education programmes delivered by university-prepared early childhood teachers, for 15 hours per week, 40 weeks of the year, in public, private and community-based pre-schools and childcare. This initiative will be supported by the development of the Early Years Learning Framework emphasising play-based learning, early literacy and numeracy skills and social development, supported by National Quality Standards for Child Care and Preschool (Department for Children, Schools and Families 2009). Universal access is be achieved by 2013. A Home Interaction Program will assist disadvantaged three- to five-year-olds in 50 communities by providing home tutors, books and associated educational resources to help parents improve their children's school readiness.

These initiatives should be welcomed not only by the teaching profession. but by all those interested in promoting individual and communal well-being in our country. The alternative to investing in early childhood education and care is to live with the cruel hypocrisy of expecting and accepting early school departures, followed by heavy investments in the state agencies that in various ways regulate the behaviour of people ill-equipped to face the challenges of contemporary society. A career that has criss-crossed the lives of families in disadvantaged communities and their children's assignment to human disposal units of various kinds has made me acutely aware of this wretched life trajectory. What an improvement it would be – morally, economically – to do something serious about challenging the inter-generational transmission of poverty and limited education that continues to help shape the destinies of significant numbers of our children. The Australian government's early education and care programme is a serious first step, but remembering the degree of deprivation experienced by the children that I encountered in pre-schools and kindergartens serving highly disadvantaged areas, certain focused additional provisions are required.

Conclusion

The same needs exist in many other countries that have yet to give early education and care the priority needed to ensure that all children achieve educationally and avoid entrapment in social disadvantage. States sharing that ambition should, firstly, follow the example of countries like Sweden and the UK and, in localities marked by high degrees of cumulative social disadvantage, provide a quantum of guaranteed pre-school for children in the two years prior to formal schooling. Within Australia national government agencies and a social policy advisory body, the Australian Social Inclusion Board, have acquired considerable facility in identifying the areas in question (Australian Social Inclusion Board 2008).

Secondly, contemporary states should recognise the need for pre-school support services in areas such as speech, hearing, vision and behavioural difficulties, so that timely interventions can be made when problems are most open to correction. My experience in this regard has been confined to one country, Australia, but the evidence presented has been of such consistency and strength as to place the identified needs high on any country's checklist of issues to be reviewed. If there has been one consistent message from the pre-schools and kindergartens visited and observed it has been the difficulty, bordering on impossibility, of obtaining speech therapy services for children in need of such help. While the *assessment* of speech difficulties is sometimes manageable, an 18-months wait for therapeutic intervention negates the whole intent of laying down a good foundation for formal schooling. Many principals and teachers believe that the only sure way forward is to locate speech pathologists within clusters of schools so that they can provide necessary direct services to children in need of that help and work in a concentrated way as partners with early childhood educators.

Unless we are reconciled to a future in which some individuals have disadvantage piled upon disadvantage from the beginning of their lives and an ever-increasing number of human disposal institutions to contain the inevitable consequences, we will insist on a high-quality and adequately funded approach to the early education of all of our children. Our generation should not be remembered for the number of jails that we bequeath. It could be remembered for rescuing the souls of our most vulnerable children from the darkness that Victor Hugo lamented. Our sense of justice, our obligations to all of our children demand nothing less. Early childhood education and care must be a priority in every country that aspires to be counted among the civilised nations.

References

Australian Bureau of Statistics (2004) Australian social trends. 15 June. http://www.abs
.gov.au/Ausstats/abs@.nsf/0/30edac9d34afc189ca256e9e0028706f?OpenDocument
(accessed 10 March 2009).

Australian Social Inclusion Board (2008) Record of the meeting of the Board on 19
November.   http://www.deewr.gov.au/Department/SocialInclusion/Documents
/BoardMeetingrecord19Nov08.pdf (accessed 24 June 2009).

Barnett, S., Brown, K., Shore, R. (2004) The universal vs. targeted debate: Should the
United States have preschool for all? *Preschool Policy Matters* 6, April: 1-16.

Department for Children, Schools and Families (2009) The national strategies.
http://nationalstrategies.standards.dcsf.gov.uk/earlyyears (accessed 14 February 2009)

Dickinson, D. and Tabors, P. (eds.) (2001) *Beginning Literacy with Language: Young
Children Learning at Home and School*. Baltimore: Brookes Publishing.

ECCD Briefs (1999) Calculating cost savings: The High/Scope Perry Pre-School Project.
http://www.ecdgroup.com/download/bh1ccshu.pdf (accessed 7 May 2009).

Elkind, D. (1986) Formal education and early childhood education: an essential
difference. *Phi Delta Kappan* 67 (9): 631-36.

Entwisle, D., Alexander, K. and Olson, L., (2005) First grade and educational attainment
by age 22: a new story. *American Journal of Sociology* 110: 1458-1502.

ESTIA (2003) Pre-school education in Sweden. http://www.estia.educ.goteborg.se/sv-
estia/edu/edu_sys2.html (accessed 17 November 2008).

Friendly, M. and Lero, D. (2002) *Social Inclusion through Early Childhood Education
and Care*. Toronto: Laidlaw Foundation.

Human Early Learning Partnership (2006) CONTEXT MATTERS: Examining the early
literacy skills and developmental health of kindergartens. British Columbia University,
April.   http://www.excellence-jeunesenfants.ca/documents/Lesaux_posterANG
.pdf#search=%22Examining%20the%20early%20literacy%20skills%20and%20
developmental%20health%20of%20kindergartens%22 (accessed 20 March 2009).

Karoly, L., Kilburn, R. and Cannon, J. (2005) *Early Childhood Interventions: Proven
Results, Future Promise*. Santa Monica: RAND Corporation.

Lynch, R. (2004) *Exceptional Returns: Economic, Fiscal and Social Benefits of
Investment in Early Childhood Development*. Washington, DC: Economic Policy
Institute.

Marcon, R. (2002) Moving up the grades: relationship between preschool model and later
school success. *Early Childhood Research and Practice* 4 (1), Urbana-Champaign,
University of Illinois Clearinghouse on Early Education and Parenting http://ecrp
.uiuc.edu/v4n1/marcon.html (accessed 20 October 2008).

National Agency for School Improvement (2007) Swedish education. http://www.sweden
.se/eng/Home/Education/Facts/Swedish-education/ (accessed 17 May 2009).

NSW Department of Community Services (2002) *The Practice of Relationships: Essential
Provisions for Children's Services*. Sydney: Office of Childcare.

OECD (2001a) Starting strong – early childhood education and care, (executive summary),
France. http://www.childcarecanada.org/pubs/pdf/startingstrong.pdf (accessed 16
April 2009).

OECD (2001b) An overview of ECEC systems in the participating countries. *OECD Country Note*. http://www.oecd.org/dataoecd/44/17/1942377.pdf (accessed 2 February 2009).

OFSTED (2006) National standards for day care. http://www.dorsetsurestart.gov.uk /OFSTEDNational_Standards.aspx?navid=324 (accessed 15 July 2009).

OFSTED (2007) Early years: getting on well. http://www.ofsted.gov.uk/Ofsted-home/Publications-and-research/Browse-all-by/Education/Pre-school-learning/Early-years-Getting-on-well/(language)/eng-GB (accessed 7 July 2010).

Schneider, J., Avis, M. and Leighton, P. (eds.) (2007) *Supporting Children and Families: Lessons from Sure Start for Evidence based Practice in Health, Social Care and Education*. London: Jessica Kingsley.

Schweinhart, Lawrence J., Montie, Jeanne, Xiang, Zongping, Barnett, William S., Belfield, Clive R. and Nores, Milagros (2005) *Lifetime Effects: The High/Scope Perry Preschool Study through Age 40*. Ypsilanti: High/Scope Press.

Skolverket (2005) The Swedish National Agency for Education. http://www.skolverket.se /sb/d/353 (accessed 14 May 2009).

Smith, M. and Dickinson, D. (2002) *Early Language and Literacy Classroom Observation Toolkit*. Baltimore: Brookes Publishing

Starr, A. (2002) The Importance of Teaching Tots. *Business Week*, August: 164.

Uniting Care Burnside, SDN Children's Services and Uniting Care Children's Services (2005) *A Good Start for Children – Integrated Child and Family Services in Australia*. Sydney: Uniting Care Burnside (report prepared by Jennifer Pannell).

Notes

[1] **Tony Vinson** is an honorary professor, Faculty of Education and Social Work, at the University of Sydney, and emeritus professor at the University of New South Wales. Trained originally as a social worker, Vinson has been a parole officer and, later, head of the NSW prison system. He has a strong background experience of working with some of the most disadvantaged members of Australian society and throughout his career has maintained an active life of research into social disadvantage. He is the author of *Dropping off the Edge: The Distribution of Disadvantage throughout Australia* (Melbourne: Jesuit Social Services/ Catholic Social Services Australia, 2007) and with K. Esson and K. Johnston, *Public Education in New South Wales: The Vinson Inquiry* (Sydney: Pluto Press, 2002). He is the principal author of a publication by the Australian Government's Social Inclusion Board, *A Compendium of Social Inclusion Indicators* (Canberra: Department of Prime Minister and Cabinet, 2009).

7   The experience of Youth Off The Streets

Father Chris Riley with Karelynne Randall[1]

Introduction

This chapter gives an account of the Youth Off The Streets programme, which I commenced in Sydney in 1991. Youth Off The Streets is a community organisation working for young people who suffer from one or more of several problems: they may be chronically homeless, drug dependent, recovering from abuse and/ or long term disengaged from schooling, and as a result they are abjectly disadvantaged. We support these young people as they work to turn their lives around and overcome immense personal traumas caused by neglect and physical, psychological and emotional abuse. The programme is strongly committed to the principle that all such youth are capable of rehabilitation. One essential aspect of their rehabilitation will be participation in effective educational activity, and we recognise that literacy is a necessary resource to help them achieve an adequate education and develop into independent responsible beings.

The image in Figure 1 represents the Circle of Courage adopted by Youth Off The Streets, revealing the core values that underpin of all our work.

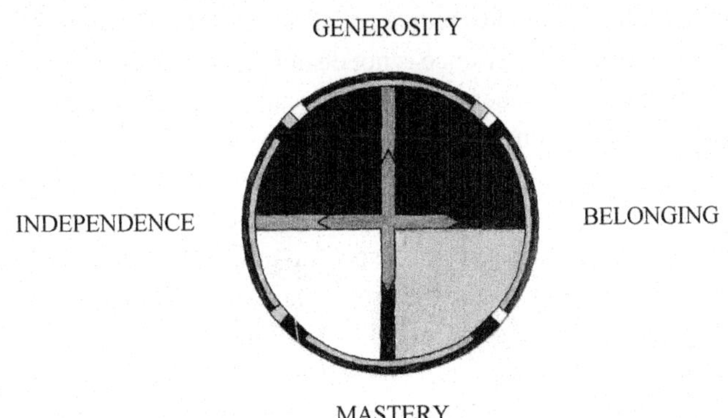

Figure 1. The Circle of Courage

The Circle of Courage embodies four core values for nurturing all children in a climate of respect and dignity (Brendtro *et al.* 1992). The model is intended to suggest to teachers principles to guide development of effective relationships, and it is based on some fundamental assumptions, to be explained briefly below before going on to outline how the teaching programme is implemented.

1. **The spirit of belonging**: the universal longing for human bonds is nurtured by relationships of trust so that the young person can say, 'I am loved'.
2. **The spirit of mastery**: the young person's inborn thirst for learning is nurtured; learning to cope with the world, the young person can say, 'I can succeed'.
3. **The spirit of independence**: the young person's free will is nurtured by increased responsibility so that the young person can say, 'I have power to make decisions'.
4. **The spirit of generosity**: the young person's character is nurtured by concern for others so that the child can say, 'I have a purpose for my life'.

Youth Off The Streets devises education support programmes for students because of the importance of education generally, and literacy in particular, in the lives of troubled young people. Education is their way out of the cycle of poverty and abuse. It is well known that the longer you keep young people at school, the more likely they are able to pull their lives together. For example, when I first met with a group of Aboriginal elders in a small community, I asked them what would be the most important thing we could offer their young people. In unison the answer was, 'Teach our kids to read – then they will be able to get jobs and do something with their lives'. Whilst we recognise the importance of teaching and learning literacy in relation to troubled teenagers, however, we must also acknowledge the interconnectedness of all aspects of young people's lives. If the trauma young people experience is not dealt with, no serious learning can be achieved. The assumptions underpinning our educational programmes are therefore crucial to establishing an environment that opens young people up to learning.

For example, the short scenario below illustrates my first encounter with a student new to our programme. One day I entered a classroom and suggested to the students that they should start their spelling task. All the students knew the routine and were comfortable with the process apart from one boy. He was a new student, 14 years of age and 6 feet tall. He turned to me and told me 'my programmes were ****** and I could go and get ****'. I informed him that this was not a jail and that if he didn't want to be here he could go and pack his bags. He stormed off, and I reflected on my old reliable saying, 'Behaviour is language'. What was his behaviour trying to communicate? Reading his file, it became very clear what he was saying to me. I read that at the age of eight this little bloke saw his father shoot his mother dead. The father then turned the gun on himself and killed himself in front of the boy. His father had sexually assaulted him from the age of three to eight. Since the death of his family, he had been in 35 different placements – we were number 36.

His language was telling me, 'Go to hell, I don't trust any of you adults and why should I, because the very people who should have loved me are dead?' His language was also making a clear statement: 'Are you going to kick me out if I don't play by the rules?' Informed by the work of Rogers and Connor (both quoted in Edwards and Watts 2008), I understood that this student was disrupting the learning context because of his dysfunctional history. His misbehaviour was a 'form of communication' and I needed to be careful not to misinterpret the student's intended meaning. This is just one example, and there are many valid causes of a young person's unhappy behaviour. Moreover, there are many opportunities within the work of Youth Off The Streets to make a difference for such young people.

Some fundamental assumptions behind the Youth Off The Streets programme

There are at least eight fundamental assumptions that underpin the strategies and interventions adopted in Youth Off The Streets, some drawn from psychological theory, others from pedagogical and curriculum theory, and some informed by restorative justice issues and theory.

The first important assumption states that there is no such thing as a child born bad. Children's behaviour and views of the world are shaped by key circles of influence, involving family, peers, school and the community, and children may learn to behave badly where such influences are negative. The psychologist, Bronfenbrenner (2005) asserts that trusting bonds with children are the most powerful force in building healthy brains and behaviour. Using the notion of 'attachment theory' (Bowlby 1969), we argue that children need a sense of strong emotional attachment to another person, ideally a parent. The central theme of attachment theory is that mothers who are available and responsive to their infants' needs establish a sense of security. The infant knows that the caregiver is dependable, which creates a secure base for the child to explore the world (Howe 2005). Troubled youth who enter specialist programmes such as Youth Off The Streets often do not have that attachment. Therefore the school must try to establish an environment of trust, building rapport, so that young people are saturated in stability of routine, consistency of expectation, and use of integrated and repeated intervention strategies. The aim of these strategies is to create up-front tasks, with consistent and constructive feedback so that students actively decide to engage and re-engage in productive learning (Howard 2006).

A second important assumption in our programme concerns the importance of inclusiveness. Where children have been chronically disengaged from education for a myriad of reasons for exceptionally long periods of time, they display marked disadvantage and are often unable to utilise, or even engage in, mainstream education. To support these exceptional children, we seek to achieve inclusiveness, drawing in both young people with learning difficulties and those who are described as gifted, but who also need some modification made to the curriculum or the pedagogy in dealing with them (Heward 2006). Within this approach, the class teacher must assume prime responsibility and must coordinate related services with such people as specialist teachers, psychologists, case workers, youth workers and providers of accommodation (Heward 2006).

A third assumption concerns the use of a 'strength based approach' (Seligman and Peterson 2003). This involves working with the strengths – traits or qualities – found in students, and exploiting them in their learning. While strengths are said to be internal and particular to individuals, they will emerge and develop with the support of teachers, who will encourage students to use them, gaining stability and resilience in their learning (Wolin and Wolin 1993). In contrast to deficit models of intervention, the strength-based model seeks to identify students' positive features in order to facilitate their ongoing development. The advantage of the strength-based approach is that teachers are expected to work with the unique qualities of all children (Graham and Slee 2005) within regular classes. Researchers have shown that learners are more likely to engage deeply in learning if they believe that learning has some potential value and purpose for them (Barton 1992) and if they are free from anxiety (Cambourne and Turbill 1991). Therefore re-engaging disaffected young people is the key to their learning. The emphasis for the school and its teachers is to support the disengaged youths in the programme through individual planning and to enable them to reconnect with learning through meaningful educational experiences.

A fourth assumption concerns youths' behaviour and the need to see bad behaviour as evidence of stress and pain. Where youths exhibit bad behaviour, this tells us a great deal about how they think and view the world (Bandura 1986). Connor (in Edwards and Watts 2008) discussing pain, argued that, as far as learning was concerned, there was little difference between the effect of physical pain and psychological pain. Both types of pain are debilitating and inhibit learning. The pain model recognises that social problems such as homelessness, lack of skills, depression, domestic violence, abuse and addiction cause psychological pain, as do organic problems, such as autism spectrum disorder (ASD) or Attention Deficit Hyperactivity Disorder (ADHD). The base assumption of the pain model is that if students feel good, they will 'act good', and so, conversely, if students feel bad, they will act badly. The model was envisaged to assist teachers who work with students who have extremely challenging behaviours, social problems and a lack of social skills. Punishment in these circumstances will only exacerbate the problem. The pain model works off the assumption that human behaviour is one way of communicating inner feelings. Literally, the behaviour is language and it's up to the adult/educator in the interaction not to react, but to interpret sensitively, respond and re-direct toward positive engagement. Here it is essential for the teacher to try to build authentic, caring, supportive and trusting relationships. By acknowledging the student's pain, the teacher begins the often slow process of developing a connection to the student – the first step to valuing that person. It must be assumed that students can learn to govern themselves with assistance. We actively communicate that they have choices, are capable of overcoming issues and problems with support, and can make decisions for which they are ultimately responsible.

Our experience has often been that adults give up at the first sign of conflict with unhappy youths, reinforcing their view of themselves as worthless and broken. Yet we believe that all young people deserve to relate positively and engage productively with others. This means they must learn to allow themselves to let go of the pain of past experiences. In the Youth Off The Streets programme young people can learn to let go of painful experiences because of our chosen practices and procedures. Thus, we do not assume that our students will change immediately, or that they will have immediate or conscious recognition of changes in their own behaviour, as these occur over time. This is understandable, given their history. However, the evidence of such changes, as is revealed in participation in positive conversation, active engagement in assessment tasks and classroom activities, and in interviews, encourages us to believe they can, and will, change. As good behaviour emerges and develops, this is recognised and supported by the teachers, so that the youths receive positive reinforcement in their learning.

A fifth assumption concerns the curriculum and the need to make connections with the background, interests and experiences of the students who enter the programme. Thus, young people are engaged in learning through integrated units of study involving meaningful tasks, which subtly coerce the learners to draw upon and apply the skills of reading, writing and doing. Cambourne's conditions of learning (2000) are environmental conditions for teaching and learning employed at EDEN, in conjunction with select literacy strategies that actively enhance effective reading, writing and engagement in relevant curriculum content. These develop skills in students of a kind that is required for academic and lifelong learning. The conditions, relevant for learning language and literacy in particular, stress:

- *immersion* in using relevant language as an aspect of learning;
- *teacher demonstration* of tasks or activities;

- *engagement of learners* with what is demonstrated with plenty of practical experience being provided;
- *teacher establishment* of clear expectations about behaviour and about learning, so that learners are scaffolded towards successful social, emotional and academic development;
- *assumption of responsibility* for their learning by learners;
- *use of approximations* in learning, so that learners are encouraged to use language and literacy, even when they are not completely in control of them, and that they are encouraged to persevere and to practise till they become more confident;
- *active employment* in tasks so that students have the benefit of constant practice;
- and *teacher response* that is positive and constructive.

A sixth assumption is that teachers must seek to inspire young people to believe that they can contribute to their family, community and wider world. They can make a difference. A seventh assumption – really evident in all the earlier assumptions – stresses the importance of teachers seeking to establish positive relationships with the youths (Howard 2005), so that effective communication can develop.

An eighth assumption concerns the importance of restorative justice in developing a sense of responsible participation in society. In *Crime, Shame and Reintegration*, Australian criminologist John Braithwaite (1989) posited that society's most potent normative force is the influence of our closest family and friends. He found that in societies with the lowest crime rates, such as Japan, communities rely on formal and informal processes by which those affected by crime can express their disapproval to offenders, while also offering opportunities for reintegration (Braithwaite 1989). In this sense, such societies offer restorative justice. The restorative alternatives utilise social connectedness and relationships to internalise social norms and healthy behaviour. Individuals are empowered to play an active role in the decisions that affect them most while strengthening connection to those around them (Brendtro *et al.* 1992). From this perspective the primary goal of restorative environments is to foster social discipline. Within the restorative framework, power is defined as the ability to influence the community through control of one's own behaviour and participation in collective processes (Brendtro *et al.* 1992). Restorative environments can reclaim anti-social individuals because they satisfy our innate need to establish self-worth and exert influence over our environment. Restorative cultures apply communal pressure to change behaviour by utilising relationships and social connection in lieu of force and coercion. Punishment is transformed into 'social consequences' – the need to confront the impact that one's behaviour has on others (Brendtro and Larson 2006). Our teachers/staff and associates attempt to become significant others in young people's environment through their engagement in community-based projects run through Youth Off The Streets. These projects involve students working in such areas as childcare, hospitality, maritime boat building and aged care, as they build new relationships and self-esteem through their efforts. A case study of one of these projects, known as the Lizard Project, is described below, involving students using their developing literacy skills in working with young children.

The Lizard Project: Service Learning at EDEN

Service Learning is an innovative values-based intervention programme, which aims to teach young people generosity and empathy for others – putting values into action. Service Learning projects enable students to translate their everyday learning into meeting real community requirements by identifying local needs and working to address them. Youth Off The Streets runs some of its intervention programmes, such as the Lizard Project, through its Education Development Empowerment Now (EDEN) Learning Centre in the Sydney suburb of Macquarie Fields. This project was devised to provide literacy support for young children, and the exercise combined service to a targeted group in a specific community (i.e. the young children) with learning for the adolescent students from Youth Off The Streets. The project sought to re-engage the youth in the productive use of language and literacy within and beyond the classroom by involving them in a highly effective literacy intervention and enrichment programme.

The project was named after the fictional lizards in the book *Holes* (Sachar 1998). The novel was first read to the secondary students as a way of engaging them in literacy practices. Through this introduction to the novel, the students, who were exceptionally reluctant to engage in any reading, became fascinated by the characteristics and physical traits of the lizards. The teacher at the EDEN centre capitalised on this interest and encouraged students to draw and paint lizards to link the students into the descriptive language used by the author. This knowledge later became the basis on which the high school students were able to work with pre-school children. Lizards was chosen as a suitable topic to work with as the children from the local pre-school were investigating lizards in their own environment.

During the Lizard Project the secondary students revisited and re-learned specific early language and literacy strategies to prepare them to work with young children as part of their service to the community. As additional motivation for their work, the students were given the information that approximately 29 out of 35 pre-schoolers, in certain demographic areas, had already suffered significant

Figure 2. Youth Off The Streets students, Ben and others, interview pre-schoolers about lizards with support from their teacher Karelynne

developmental language delay on entry to pre-school. Students developed appropriate pro-social communication and presentation skills to interview pre-school children and record their knowledge about lizards.

Information was collected and then used to produce a children's factual text about lizards based on the young child's own language. Through the Lizard Project the secondary students learned how to read to young children, learning to adopt and model good practices for reading to the young. This process was intended to be of support to the parents, as first educators of their children. This project helped the parents of the children, while it also enhanced the language and literacy competences of both groups of students. Overall, the project enhanced the ability of the young people to understand the uses of age-appropriate texts. The experience also strengthened their self-esteem and improved their sense of social acceptance.

The secondary students who were involved in the Lizard Project all responded positively as they were appreciated as productive members of the community. They were accountable for their work, became confident and were happy to take part in the process. They also understood that they were gaining useful work-related skills that they could transfer and use in some employment situations such as childcare.

Figure 3. Youth Off The Streets student, Jess, reading her lizard book to pre-school children

Other Service Learning projects run through Youth Off The Streets include the Walking in my Shoes Camp for Children with Disabilities, The Brumbies Wild Horses Programme and the East Timor Service Learning Project. Walking in my Shoes involves a series of three-day camps for children with disabilities, where young people from Youth Off The Streets deliver a specially designed, fun-filled activity camp for the children, which helps them understand the importance and value of being caring and generous to others. The Brumbies Wild Horses Programme was used to encourage young people to learn a way of communicating that is based on trust and respect, rather than violence. They did this by training wild, endangered horses (called brumbies), guided by a professional horse handler. The East Timor Service Learning Project gives students the experience of working with orphans in impoverished contexts in East Timor. The students from Youth Off The Streets have often faced similar vulnerability through sexual assault or rejection by their families, and they have sometimes overcome histories of drug abuse, physical assault and poverty. However, through spending time with the East Timorese orphans, they see that they can make a difference in this world and that they can contribute. Moreover, they can overcome their own pain through learning to be generous to others. Ensuing Service Learning projects have continued to be strengthened through a focus upon actual workplace competencies, in direct relation to the particular industry in which students are involved, or wish to become involved, such as aged care, hospitality or boat building.

Entry to programmes

Students referred to Youth Off The Streets range in age from approximately 14 to 18 years, and the years involved cover the secondary school years from year 8 to year 12. The referrals are the result of a well-established network of community relationships, and a process of continual communication, with groups such as: school principals and counsellors, NSW Department of Juvenile Justice case workers, police youth liaison officers, NSW Department of Education home school liaison officers, NSW Department of Community Services representatives, representatives of Technical and Further Education (TAFE) colleges in NSW, mental health services as well as parents, extended family and community members.

Parents or guardians are provided with a referral pack prior to an initial interview, to collate comprehensive information about students' home and family situations, physical and mental health, welfare and educational background. Such information is used by staff in making preliminary decisions about the best steps to take in ensuring students' well-being. Assessment of students' needs is of course a very important part of the whole process, and trained staff work with the initial information they receive. Students are referred to the EDEN Centre, where staff members examine the completed referral package in preparing for an initial interview with a youth and a family member or guardian. At the initial interview, an effort is made to establish our policy of offering no judgements about past actions, focusing instead on future activity and prospects. The intention is to establish a new, more positive attitude towards schooling. This is the point at which the building of rapport with staff commences (Howard 2005). Youths are encouraged to discuss future opportunities, and to consider the suitability for their needs of our different educational programmes. Youth Off The Streets runs accredited high schools, which offer a flexible curriculum with a focus on literacy and numeracy that responds to the specific needs, interests and talents of young people who have become disconnected from mainstream education. At our schools, such as Key College, Chapel School and Mathew Hogan School, general education is available for years 8–12 and at the EDEN Learning Centre for years 8–10. Through their connection with these learning opportunities, increasing numbers of students go on to achieve their School Certificate (at the end of year 10), their Higher School Certificate (at the end of year 12) or various vocational pathways programmes through courses at TAFE NSW and other providers of vocational education and training.

After a discussion of educational possibilities, as part of building the rapport and some trust at this early stage, youths are invited to attend a further appointment, so that a more detailed assessment of their needs can be made. Subsequent assessment procedures are intended to reinforce a sense of self-worth in youths, by identifying as positively as possible what they can do, as well as what they need to learn. Oral language, literacy and numeracy skills are all assessed, while the staff member tries to establish any behavioural patterns in youths that may have previously interfered with their learning, such as engaging in deliberately disruptive actions in the classroom. The behaviour is discussed with a view to persuading the youths to change it in the new classroom environment to be provided. Once the initial assessment is finished, the results are used as a benchmark for the design of a holistic Individual Learning Plan (ILP) for each youth. This ILP is then used at enrolment and at later stages in a youth's progress, contributing to the development of a student portfolio.

To carry out the most effective ILP, the total well-being of the student is paramount, and with the permission of parents and carers our teachers engage general practitioners for initial medical assessment with the option of further referral. This gives the student access to the expertise of a wide range of specialists to attend to physical, mental/emotional and psychological needs, initiating a longer term holistic support framework. Using the ILP, teaching staff collaboratively select specific teaching methods and strategies to extend language and literacy learning. Due to long periods of disengagement from schooling, many students require rapid up-skilling by teaching them 'learning to learn strategies' in order to understand basic knowledge, and methods for acquiring the knowledge, such as reading. These methods are crucial to fast-track learning and to assist youths to engage successfully with learning in the various content areas, or Key Learning Areas, as established by the NSW Board of Studies.

Language enrichment is an essential aspect of the teaching programmes, achieved through daily participation of students in such activities as: guided and supported reading sessions; immersion in a wide range of reading practices, involving text prediction, among other things, as an aspect of reading; active discussion of interesting content in what is read and written about; teacher demonstration, modelling and scaffolding of well-structured and socially acceptable oral language and written texts. Such activities, among other things, provide a scaffold to engage students in active listening. This in turn enables them, again under guidance, to develop note-taking strategies, which are useful in researching and recording information to expand upon and produce complex and conventionally presented written texts. Students are taught a metalanguage and instructed in strategies for learning about language and literacy (Clay 2005). Concepts are introduced, revised, repeated and built upon at all phases of development, so that students gain ownership of such strategies, and are empowered to extend upon and re-use them independently for self advancement.

We argue that regular consistency of application by teachers of familiar and effective language of instruction is essential for teachers to assist behavioural change in their students (Howard 2006). Where students are encouraged to pay attention to what can become familiar procedures and strategies for using language in reading, writing, speaking or listening, they develop skills in recalling and interpreting information, responding critically where needed, and becoming confident in answering assignment and examination questions. Previous coping mechanisms, such as defensive and reactive behaviour, become somewhat redundant and/or unnecessary when students are surrounded with respectful behaviour, and where a sense of responsibility is encouraged and expected. One result is that students have a sense of safety in risk taking as they learn practical new strategies in a safe and supportive environment.

Once accepted into the programme, students attend classes according to the appropriate learning context chosen for them. Beginning with the initial assessment results, teachers commence work with the youths, and they regularly monitor their progress, keeping a record of their achievements, including a portfolio of work samples. Evidence of progress is gathered through various means, such as observation in classrooms, collection of anecdotal records in writing, and video-taped records of students providing practical demonstrations of their knowledge through spoken delivery, while samples of texts they write are also collected. Students' progress is thus monitored in a variety of ways.

Teachers, students, parents and/or parent representatives attend regular reviews of each student's ILP in order to maintain an appropriate learning direction and ensure the ongoing social adaptation of the student. When students sit for examinations set by the state's Board of Studies, such as the School Certificate at year 10, and the Higher School Certificate at year 12, the results are used to inform our overall programme design for future practices. The programme is thus subject to constant review, adaptation and amendment.

Students enter our overall programme relatively late in their school years, and every effort is made to keep them within it, so that they can successfully complete a secondary school education. While they remain with us, seeking to complete their academic training, we make every endeavour to ensure the youths make adequate progress emotionally and socially, so that they can be judged ready to enter further study and/or employment when they leave us.

The overall success of the programme

A decade of experience has taught us that education is the most effective way to break the cycles of abuse and poverty that can trap young people. The success of our programmes is evidenced in a number of areas, such as a marked increase in student attendance, a range of portfolios of educational and personal success, some inclusive of various recognitions awarded by community agencies and state and nationally accredited agencies. All such evidence is testament to our belief that the disadvantaged youth of our society have the propensity to change and the potential to learn and become independent, personally and socially responsible individuals.

Our literacy programmes are succeeding, in that increasing numbers of disaffected youths are helped to turn their lives around and to develop the necessary literate skills for effective participation in the workplace and the wider society. Such literacy programmes will only be effective if they take into account the trauma and the total ecology of young people's lives. The building of good strong relationships is at the basis of successful teaching and learning. We have highlighted throughout this chapter some strategies we use to build respectful alliances with young people.

References

Bandura, A. (1986) *Social Foundations of Thought and Action: A Cognitive Theory.* Englewood Cliffs, NJ: Prentice Hall.

Barton, B. (1992) *An Evaluation of 'Teacher-as-Co Researcher' as a Methodology for Staff Development.* Wollongong: University of Wollongong.

Bowlby, J. (1969) *Attachment and loss.* I. *Separation: Anxiety and Anger.* New York: Russell Sage Foundation.

Braithwaite, J. (1989) *Crime, Shame and Reintegration.* New York: Cambridge University Press.

Brendtro, L., Brokenleg, M. and Van Bockern, S. (1992) *Reclaiming Youth at Risk: Our Hope for the Future.* Bloomington, IN: National Educational Services.

Brendtro, L. and Larson, S. (2006) *The Resilience Revolution: Discovering Strengths in Challenging Kids.* Bloomington, IN: Solution Tree.

Bronfenbrenner, U. (2005) *Making Human Beings Human: Human Biological Perspectives on Human Development.* Thousand Oaks, CA: Sage Publications.

Cambourne, B. (2000) Toward an ecologically relevant theory of literacy learning: twenty years of inquiry. In N.D. Padak, T.V. Rasinski, J.K. Peck, B. Church, G. Fawcett, J. Hendershot, J.M. Henry, B. Moss, E. Pryor, K.A. Roskos, J.F. Baumann, D.R. Dillon, C.J. Hopkins, J.W. Humphrey and D.G. O'Brien (eds.) *Distinguished Educators on Reading.* Newark, DE: International Reading Association, 47-66.

Cambourne, B. and Turbill, J. (1991) Teacher-as-co researcher: How an approach to research became a methodology for staff development. In J. Turbill, A. Butler and B. Cambourne (eds.), *Frameworks: A Whole Language Staff Development Program.* New York: Wayne-Fingerlakes BOCES, 3-8.

Clay, M. (2005) *Literacy Lessons Designed for Individuals: Why? When? and How?,* I. Auckland: Heinemann.

Edwards, C. and Watts, V. (2008) *Classroom Discipline and Management*. Milton, QLD: John Wiley & Sons.

Graham, L. and Slee, R. (2005) Inclusion. Paper presented at the Australian Association for Research in Education, Sydney.

Heward, W. (2006) *Exceptional Children: An Introduction to Special Education*, 8th edn. Ohio: Pearson.

Howard, C. (2005) *Results Certification Training*. Manhattan Beach, CA: Christopher Howard Training.

Howard, C. (2006) *Master Results Training*. Manhattan Beach, CA: Christopher Howard Training.

Howe, D. (2005) *Child Abuse and Neglect: Attachment, Development and Intervention*. New York: Palgrave McMillan.

Sachar, L. (1998) *Holes*. New York: Farrar, Straus & Giroux.

Seligman, M. and Peterson, C. (2003) Positive clinical psychology. In L. Aspinwall and U. Staudinger (eds.) *A Psychology of Human Strengths: Fundamental Questions and Future Directions for a Positive Psychology*. Washington, DC: American Psychological Association.

Wolin, S. and Wolin, S. (1993) *The Resilient Self: How Survivors of Troubled Families Rise above Adversity*. New York: Villard Books.

Notes

[1] Wherever the chapter uses 'I', this refers to Father Chris Riley. Details of Youth Off The Streets are available at the website: www.youthoffthestreets.com.au

Father Chris Riley is the founder and CEO of Youth Off The Streets, a programme initiated in the Australian state of New South Wales, though Riley has by now an international reputation for his work. He has worked with disadvantaged youth for more than 30 years in a variety of roles including teacher, youth worker, probation officer, residential carer and principal. He has particular interests in the provision of literacy programmes to help the most disadvantaged.

Karelynne Randall is a senior teacher at Father Chris Riley's Youth Off The Streets EDEN Learning Centre. She has more than 30 years experience working in infants, primary, secondary, TAFENSW youth and adult education designing and implementing language- and literacy-based educational and vocational programmes. Her passion is engaging students in language development, enhancing literacy skills and facilitating competent and confident communication.

Key College, Macquarie Fields Campus – is the registered name of the school named in the chapter as the EDEN Centre.

8   Beating educational inequality with an integrated reading pedagogy

David Rose[1]

The Pitjantjatjara experience

In the 1980s a great social movement was sweeping remote Indigenous communities in Australia, in which families were leaving the government settlements and missions of the assimilation era, and taking their children home to their ancestral lands. As part of this 'homelands movement', I worked for many years for the Pitjantjatjara people of central Australia. To be able to work for such a great ideal was an honour and an inspiration, as well as a steep educational experience, learning how to interact in a very different culture, to speak a different language, and to raise a family in the harsh conditions of desert living and working. But I was fortunate to have some of the greatest teachers and role models anyone could hope for – the Pitjantjatjara elders who were the leaders of the homelands movement.

Sounds idyllic, doesn't it? But cast across this bright picture, of a great future in the making, was a terrifying dark shadow. The entire teenage generation of Pitjantjatjara children were destroying themselves in an orgy of petrol sniffing. To give an idea of how awful that was, it was not just the constant stink of petrol fumes that gangs of children inhaled from tin cans held permanently to their faces, or the ghoulish, often violent behaviour the drug induced, but the lead in the petrol was stripping their neurones, turning intelligent children into cripples, and killing them one by one. In some communities 80 per cent of children from 12 to 20 were sniffing petrol all their waking hours, living in appalling squalor, terrorising their families, and demolishing the houses and infrastructure of their communities. Within my first year there I quit my job in community development and went to work voluntarily for the only people doing anything serious about this crisis, the elders who had adopted my family in the Pitjantjatjara kinship system, Nganyintja and Charlie Ilyatjari.

Together with other community leaders, Nganyintja and Charlie saw education as the long-term solution for this disaster, and took every opportunity to demand a decent school education for their children. Working on their cultural and training programme with those young people, two things were depressingly clear: none of them had more than a smattering of literacy in either Pitjantjatjara or English, and whatever education they had received had given them none of the resources they needed to cope with the changes their communities were going through, to help them construct secure identities that could handle those changes. The oblivion that petrol sniffing afforded was their way out of the confusion and lack of self-esteem that a lack of useful education had left them with.

Now all of these children had attended the state schools in their communities until at least year 6, in which the main teaching focus was a Pitjantjatjara language curriculum that was supposed to bridge them into school literacy, at the same time as helping maintain their culture, but patently achieved neither (Japangardi-Poulson 1988; Lester 1993; Rose 1992). Some children attended sporadically, particularly as they got older, but most had sat in classrooms for many hundreds of hours through their childhood years, yet had apparently learnt very little about reading, writing, numeracy, or any of the curriculum content we normally expect from primary school. How could this be, given that their teachers were trained professionals, often with specific skills in ESL and literacy in the early years?

Part of the answer was given by research such as Folds 1987, who showed that class time in Aboriginal community schools was overwhelmingly taken up with procedures, behaviour management and busywork, leaving little time for actual learning activities. The reasons for this imbalance in classroom time were partly explained by Malcolm (1991), who recorded the dysfunctional communication that is typical in Aboriginal community schools when teachers use the standard patterns of asking questions. Malcolm and others thus assumed that asking questions is a non-Aboriginal practice, which Aboriginal children reject. But this conclusion is wide of the mark: questions are a part of interactions between teachers and learners in Indigenous Australian cultures as much as in any other culture. The critical issue is whether learners can answer the questions successfully. In classrooms the world over, teachers continually ask questions that some students can answer but others cannot. We then use the responses of successful students as stepping stones in the progress of our lessons (Alexander 2000; Gibbons 2002; Nassaji and Wells 2000; Rose 2004). What happens then in classrooms where no student is able or willing to give the answers we are after? That is the situation that Malcolm and others have observed, and which forces teachers to resort to activities that have little or no learning value, as Folds observed, but which avoid the behaviour problems that result from communication failure in the classroom.

Certainly there was a problem with the standard question-response-feedback pattern of classroom interaction, but the problem was not so much with teachers asking questions, but with the children's inability to respond successfully. So why couldn't these Aboriginal children give the responses their teachers needed? One factor that was starkly apparent was that none of them could read at anything like the levels needed to engage with the primary school curriculum. In 1998 my colleagues Brian Gray, Wendy Cowey and I formally tested all the children who were present in the community schools of the Pitjantjatjara region. We found that no children were able to read independently before the end of year 3. By the end of primary only a handful could read more than basal picture books, and those that could did not understand one in every five words – they could not understand what they were reading. In the urban high school programme these children attended, few had more than junior primary level reading skills despite years of intensive one-on-one support, including help from ESL specialists (Rose, Gray and Cowey 1999).

Whatever other problems were hampering the education of these children, their inability to read the school curriculum was clearly an overwhelming stumbling block. Consequently Gray, Cowey and I made this the focus of our intervention project Scaffolding Reading and Writing for Indigenous Children in School, using reading strategies developed in the Schools and Community Centre in Canberra University, together with the genre-based approach to writing developed by Joan Rothery, Jim Martin and colleagues, with the NSW Disadvantaged Schools Program and Sydney University (Christie and Martin 1997; Rose 2008).

By the end of the project's first year, the teachers we worked with had all the high school students and many of the primary students reading at age-appropriate levels (McRae *et al.* 2000; Gray, Rose and Cowey 1998). We were able to achieve these results in one year, in just two or three lessons a week, at the same time as the teachers were figuring out how to make it work. This rapid improvement begs the question of why these children had previously remained so far behind their non-Aboriginal peers, through year after year of their schooling. One simple and unavoidable answer is that they had not been taught to read. Yet their teachers had all had the same training and professional skills as any teacher in an urban school. Their early years teachers knew the same strategies of alphabet and phonics drills, memorising 'sight words', shared, guided and individual reading, levelled reading books, letter formation, handwriting and story writing, which seemed to work, at least for the majority of urban students.

The key difference with the Pitjantjatjara children was not just that a non-English language was spoken in the home, since a high proportion of other Australian children also come from non-English speaking families, but that there was no parent–child reading in the home. International research has shown that children in literate families spend up to 1,000 hours reading with their parents before they start school (Adams 1990). Could it be that the reading strategies their early years teachers were trained in simply did not work with children who had no experience of parent–child reading in the home?

Parent–child reading gives children an orientation to written ways of meaning, and equally importantly, to the talk around text that parents and children share. This experience provides an essential foundation to the reading and interaction practices of the early years classroom. The early years literacy strategies mentioned above (most of which have been used by teachers literally for centuries) build on this orientation to meaning and interaction, so that children with this home experience rapidly learn to read independently. They can then benefit from the common practice known as individual silent reading activity, in which children choose books to read, and the teacher circulates and listens to them read aloud.

However, the consequences of this activity for some of the Pitjantjatjara children who had not learnt to read were heartbreaking to see. Through the 'sight word' strategy the children would memorise a small set of common words that they could recognise. When the teacher listened to them read a book they would say these words and stop when they got to a word they did not know, often looking up to the teacher for help. The teacher would tell them the word, which they memorised in the sequence of the sentence. After repeating this procedure several times, they would memorise most or all of the words in a simple picture book, and appear to be reading. In an astounding feat of innovation, they invented their own version of reading, and could take years to learn otherwise.

The reading curriculum

But of course it is not only Indigenous Australian children who suffer such problems with reading in school. The success achieved by the Scaffolding Reading and Writing project soon led to intense national interest, so that over the subsequent decade the programme has continually expanded with education programmes at all levels and all sectors, across Australia and internationally (Rose 2008, www.readingtolearn.com.au). What immediately became apparent in these wider contexts is that a significant proportion of students in mainstream classrooms have similar problems to the Pitjantjatjara children, and further, that many more students in all classrooms have some degree of difficulty with the reading and writing required to succeed at their education level. Despite the best efforts of junior primary teachers to provide all children with reading skills, the gap between the most and least successful students continues to widen throughout the primary and secondary years.

Children arrive at school with very different home experiences. A minority will have had the intensive experience with reading that tertiary-educated parents can give them, another large group will have had some experience with parent–

child reading, but often with less talk around text that prepares others for class-room learning, while another group will have had little or no experience of reading in the home. In a large-scale study, Williams (1999) showed consistent differences between the way that tertiary-educated and other parents read with their children, even where they spend the same amount of time doing so. From the first day of school, all children are evaluated on a hierarchy of learning 'abilities', that are framed in psychological terms, but are largely attributable to their experience of literacy in the home.

By the end of year 2, children who were well prepared by their home experi-ence are usually independently reading with understanding and engagement, while other children have acquired lesser reading skills to varying degrees. The independent readers are then ready to start developing the key skill they will need in the upper primary, that is, learning from reading. Now for young children, reading could appear a very strange form of communication, where the other person with whom we speak, laugh and generally interact is replaced by an inert object, a book that is supposed to speak to us. Likewise, in learning from reading, the person who teaches us, by modelling, explaining, guiding and praising our efforts, is replaced by an inert printed monologue that provides information or instructions.

Thus the indispensable foundation for being able to learn from reading, is to be already engaged with reading as a meaningful form of communication. But after the early years, explicit teaching of reading falls away; the focus of teaching is now more on learning the content of the curriculum, and less on the skills needed to read it. Nevertheless, almost all of the content-learning activities in the middle and upper primary involve or are associated with reading. Teachers guide their students through learning the content of their lessons, using a variety of media, but particularly printed text. This guidance enables students who are experienced readers to rapidly develop their skills in learning from reading, but children who are less experienced readers develop these skills more slowly, and will therefore be evaluated as less able learners.

By the end of primary school it is crucial to be independently learning from reading, because reading is the core mode of learning in the high school. Classroom lessons in high school prepare students for the reading-based tasks they are expected to do on their own, particularly as homework, and the lessons that follow then build on what students have learnt from their reading and associated tasks. Although the overt curriculum focus is on the content that students are expected to learn, the curriculum content is actually secondary to the underlying development of reading and writing skills. Reading and writing across the curriculum over six years of high school gives students a wealth of experience in recognising, understanding and using the language patterns of the written genres of formal education. This experience provides the foundation for the independent learning that will be required of the top 20 per cent of students when they get to university. As the teaching of reading, and how to learn from reading, is rarely an explicit part of the high school curriculum, students can only acquire these skills intuitively. To do so, they need the preparation that only those students get from primary school who have been well prepared in the home. For other students, their less adequate preparation for learning from reading in the primary school means that they will be less able to learn independently in the high school, will achieve less well in their written assessments, and will finish high school with lower grades.

The source of inequality

This system of unequal outcomes evolved in an economic context that demanded a small proportion of university trained professionals, a larger group of vocationally trained tradespeople, and a much larger proportion of workers with no further education beyond school. In Australia today these proportions of education outcomes are roughly 20:30:50 per cent, and have changed only slightly for at least the past two generations (Australian Bureau of Statistics 1994, 2004; Rose 2004, 2005). For teachers these proportions are very familiar: they correspond broadly to the proportions of students in the top, average and lower 'ability' groups in their classes, varying with the socio-economic status of the community the school serves.

It seems hardly fair that the degree of preparation that children get in the home largely determines their position on the hierarchy of success throughout their years in school, and beyond. How is it that apparently the same teaching practices and curriculum contents produce such different outcomes for different students? I have come to believe that the answer lies with the way that school dislocates the elements of learning tasks, particularly the tasks of reading and writing, and teaches them segmentally or implicitly. Students who have been adequately prepared by preceding stages in their schooling are able to intuitively recognise relations between the dislocated elements, to synthesise them as meaningful wholes, and so develop the skills they need for learning at each stage. At the same time, students who are less well prepared may take longer to recognise the relationships, and so take longer to develop the skills they need.

This problem can be illustrated with the literacy practices of the early years, which address many of the dimensions of the tasks of reading and writing, but in separate segments of the school programme, using different texts, sentences, words, sounds and letters. To appreciate why this is a problem for some students, we need to recognise the complexity of the reading and writing task, which derives from the immense complexity of language in general. For example, language operates at three levels simultaneously: patterns of meanings in texts, or discourse, which are realised as patterns of wordings in sentences, or grammar, which are realised as patterns of letters or sounds within words. To be able to understand a text, or to write one coherently, we must be able to process all these patterns of patterns of patterns simultaneously and automatically. If we are struggling in any one of these dimensions, then our capacity for processing all the others will be severely reduced.

So to teach this complexity, it must be broken down into manageable chunks and sequenced in the curriculum. In the early years this is done at the level of sound and letter patterns with alphabet and phonics activities; at the word level with 'sight word' activities; at the level of sentences, and word groups within sentences, with basal picture books that present one sentence or word group to a page; at the level of paragraphs with group reading, in which children may take turns to read each paragraph in a book; and at the level of whole texts with shared book reading, in which the teacher reads and talks through a story with the class, and with individual reading in which children choose their own books. All of these activities have been used for centuries for teaching reading, and always in some combination. The so-called literacy wars between phonics and the whole-word or whole-language methods is a phony war; all teachers employ a more or less 'balanced approach' using a variety of strategies. But the rate at which children develop reading skills from such a balanced approach varies with their experience of reading in the home.

Children with the 1,000 hours of reading and talking around text are already thoroughly prepared to understand each component of the reading task that the early years activities teach, and rapidly develop as independent readers. Children with less home reading experience have less preparation to synthesise these components, and so develop more slowly. The defining example is children with no home reading experience, such as the Pitjantjatjara children who take three or more years to read independently, from exactly the same activities, and no amount of phonics, phonemic awareness, sight word or basal reader activities has any significant impact on this learning rate.

This has nothing to do with 'intelligence' or any other psychometric measures of learning 'ability', otherwise we would have to conclude that the smartest Pitjantjatjara children are vastly less 'intelligent' or 'able' than the average urban middle-class child. Rather it is explained by the stratified nature of language, in which lower-level parts are comprehended in the context of higher-level wholes. At the lowest level, sounds and letters have no meaning, they are literally meaningless, except in the context of words that we know; but individual words only occur in the context of word groups and sentences, and each sentence is only comprehensible in the context of a whole text. In order to understand the lower-level parts of language, one must understand the higher-level contexts in which they occur. For young children this higher-level understanding is provided by parent–child reading in the home.

In the early years classroom it is shared book reading that provides such understanding, very much like parent–child reading. This is amply demonstrated in Aboriginal community schools, where early years teachers, who are typically monolingual in English, regularly enable children who have very little English to understand and say all the words in a big book, after a week or two of shared book reading. Moreover the children are typically thoroughly engaged in the story and the reading activity, by means of the warm affirming relationship with the teacher. This amazing success should form a strong foundation for them to learn to read the book themselves, but rarely does. Instead the early years literacy activities, through which they are meant to learn to read, are typically conducted with other texts, other words, other sounds and letter patterns; the lower level parts of language are dislocated from the meaningful, engaging activity of shared reading, and taught as they always have been, as discrete elements of the school curriculum programme, which such children experience as disconnected segments. Thus children who participate eagerly and intelligently in shared book reading, and experience it as a meaningful communicative activity, can come to perceive reading individually as a meaningless activity of memorising strings of words in a basal picture book.

In the upper primary and high school years we can see a comparable dislocating of elements of learning tasks, but to interpret the nature of this dislocation we need to distinguish four dimensions in the social contexts of texts: the overall social purpose of the text, or genre; its subject matter, or field; the social relations it enacts, or tenor; and the roles that language plays in realising its genre, field and tenor (Martin and Rose 2007, 2008).

In the primary school, beyond the early years, the focus of teaching is on the fields of the curriculum, and on the tenor of relationships between teacher and children, and between children. But there is a dislocation between the contents of the curriculum and the roles of language in learning those contents, particularly the role of reading. As writing is the mode in which learning is evaluated, there is some explicit focus on teaching writing, and, during the last decade in Australia, on the written genres of the primary school. But the skills that children need to learn the curriculum content, through reading, are less explicitly taught. Although whole class and group reading are common primary school practices, they are primarily focused on story reading. As they do not explicitly teach the skills that all students need, they leave different students with different levels of reading skills. Accordingly, classes are often divided into 'reading groups' according to children's assessed abilities: better readers get more challenging books to read together, others get simpler books, ensuring that they will rarely catch up to the higher reading groups.

These reading activities are conducted in separate programme segments from other activities focused on curriculum contents. As the whole class needs to learn the same contents, we may not expect the same hierarchical divisions as in story reading. Nevertheless, rather than teaching all students to read the same texts, reading materials at different levels are now being produced across primary subject areas, for students with different reading skills. As skills in learning from reading are not explicitly taught in content-focused activities, whether hierarchically divided or not, the better readers are naturally able to develop them more effectively than the weaker readers. The dislocation of reading instruction from curriculum content is then cemented in the high school, where there is much less explicit teaching of either reading or writing, despite the increasing importance and complexity of these skills from junior through to senior secondary. If the foundation for these skills has not been adequately laid in the primary, students thus have little chance of developing them in high school, and are thus doomed by the system to limited achievement.

Overcoming inequality

If the problem of unequal outcomes lies with the dislocation and segmentation of learning tasks, as I have suggested, then the solution would seem to lie with re-integrating these elements within an explicit holistic pedagogy. This is the approach we have taken over the past decade in developing the methodology now known as Reading to Learn.

In the early years this means integrating the activities that address each dimension of the reading and writing task into a unified pedagogic sequence. The starting point for this sequence is at the top of the language task, with shared book reading, as early years teachers so often use this activity brilliantly to engage children with reading, and provide the platform of understanding that is necessary to learn lower-level skills. The next step is to enable children to recognise the written words that they have learnt to say aloud in the shared reading story. This is done by showing them how to point at each word in a familiar sentence from the story as they say them aloud, supported by the sequence of words, as well as their written forms. Once they can accurately point to and say the words, various activities of cutting up and re-ordering the sentence (rewritten onto cardboard strips) are used to cement the children's recognition of both words and word groups, until they can accurately identify all its words in and out of the sentence.

This approach contrasts with the 'sight word' or 'whole word' activity traditionally used for word recognition, in which children may have weekly lists of decontextualised words to memorise, which they are then expected to recognise in books and use in their writing. The words used for memorising are often grammatical words – articles, pronouns, prepositions, conjunctions, auxiliary verbs, and so on – which are only meaningful when used together with content words in a sentence (i.e. lexical words). On their own, grammatical words are meaningless, making them harder to memorise than lexical words, especially for children with minimal reading experience.

Once children can accurately recognise the words in a sentence from the story, the next step is to cut up individual words into their letter patterns. Children are shown how to identify syllables in multisyllabic words, and then the initial consonants (or onset) of each syllable, and the remainder (or rhyme) of the syllable. As they say each letter pattern aloud, they learn to associate letter patterns and sounds, but in the context of words they already know and can say, from sentences they are familiar with. They then practise writing each letter pattern and putting them together in whole words, on small white- or blackboards.

This activity simultaneously addresses letter–sound correspondences, letter formation, handwriting and spelling. It can be contrasted with activities such as phonics programmes that begin, like the sight word activity, not with known words from familiar texts, but with decontextualised letters and digraphs, which children learn to say out of context, then put together into decontextualised words. Traditional letter formation, handwriting and spelling activities likewise use decontextualised letters and spelling words that are selected on the basis of lower-level patterns rather than higher-level meanings in familiar texts.

Once children can accurately write all the lexical or content words in a sentence, they are shown how to write the whole sentence they have been reading, at which point they practise writing the grammatical words that accompany the lexical words in the sentence. The same sequence is then repeated for the next sentences in the shared reading book, until children can independently write whole paragraphs of meaningful complex text.

This approach may be compared with learning to play a musical instrument, in which learners begin by practising tunes written by accomplished musicians, before they begin to improvise or compose their own. Here children learn the foundation skills in writing, by practising with a text written by an accomplished author. It is only when they have mastered all these dimensions of the reading and writing task that they begin writing stories of their own, and then only after the story-writing process has been carefully guided by their teacher with the whole class, closely modelled on the stories they have learnt to read. This contrasts with the widely used activity of writing from personal experience, often called journal or process writing, which is supposed to encourage children to start writing about familiar topics without requiring explicit teaching. For children with little home reading experience, the complexity of the writing task makes this activity merely discouraging, particularly for Indigenous children who typically produce short repetitive accounts throughout their primary school years, using the few words they know how to write accurately, to avoid being corrected by the teacher.

These techniques are easy to learn and easy to train teachers to use. For example, the Reading to Learn programme provides Indigenous and other teaching assistants with one day's training in the early years strategies. They then go into the classroom to practise with children who may not have learnt to read independently in three or more years of schooling, and are often diagnosed with a lack of alphabet or phonemic knowledge, or with learning disabilities. In less than one hour the teachers always have these children accurately reading sentences from shared reading books, as well as accurately spelling, forming letters and writing whole sentences. These strategies are plainly more effective than the centuries-old activities that are currently used (whatever names they may be rebadged and sold with), because they integrate and contextualise each task within higher levels of meaning. In schools undertaking Reading to Learn training, children in kindergarten to year 2, whose reading and writing has been assessed as well below the standard for their age, or at risk, consistently achieve at age-appropriate levels within two to three terms. Children who began at average levels consistently achieve above the average for their age. As a result, large-scale training programmes are now being conducted in Australia, as well as by aid agencies in east Africa and central Asia.

In the middle to upper primary and high school, re-integrating the learning task is more complex for several reasons. Firstly, teachers are often under pressure to cover a crowded curriculum in their lessons, particularly where their students do not have the reading skills to study independently. The curriculum thus appears to discourage them from taking time to teach the skills that students need to learn it. Secondly, the texts that students need to read and write are increasingly complex from year to year, and few teachers have the training in text analysis that is needed to analyse the language in these texts, in order to teach their students how to read and write it. Thirdly, all teachers are constrained by the wide range of so-called 'ability' levels in their classes. How can they advance the achievement of all their students if they spend too much time on the literacy needs of their lower achievers, which should have been met in previous years?

To address these issues, Reading to Learn uses highly designed activities known as Detailed Reading and Joint Rewriting. In Detailed Reading, key passages from curriculum texts are selected that may challenge even the top students, and the teacher guides the whole class to recognise and understand the word groups in each sentence of the passage. Students highlight the wordings as they identify them, and their understanding is then deepened by defining, explaining or discussing their meaning. This highly explicit technique enables all students to read the passage with complete understanding, and to recognise the language choices the author made in writing it. It is integrated with curriculum teaching as it deepens students' understanding of the topic they are studying, accelerating the learning of all students, at the same time as it narrows the gap between higher and lower achievers. In Joint Rewriting, the teacher then guides the class to write a new text that is patterned closely on the reading passage, using either its field content for factual texts, or its language patterns for stories and arguments. This technique cements the comprehension and language recognition skills provided by Detailed Reading, and explicitly shows students how to borrow the language resources of accomplished authors into their own writing, as all successful writers do. Detailed Reading and Rewriting are used on short text passages, but they are used in combination with strategies that prepare students for reading whole curriculum texts, and guide them to write whole texts. As they take just one or two half-hour lessons for each passage, and focus on curriculum topics, they can be readily integrated with crowded primary and secondary programmes. If this is done regularly, all students develop the skills they need for independent study within two or three school terms, allowing teachers to accelerate the pace of curriculum coverage.

As these strategies involve interacting systematically with all students in a class, around the language in a complex text, they are initially difficult to use, and always require very careful planning. To this end the Reading to Learn professional learning programme trains teachers in the educational linguistics they need to select appropriate texts in their curriculum, and to analyse them closely, to plan Detailed Reading lessons. This linguistic training also contributes to teachers' capacity for guiding students systematically in writing activities, and in analysing their students' language resources in writing assessments. To date several thousand teachers have been trained across Australia and internationally.

As in the early years, their students' results are consistently double to more than four times the learning rates expected with standard current teaching practices (Culican 2006). Figure 1 shows writing improvements for the 2008 training programme, involving around 90 schools in NSW. Results are averaged across year 1 to year 8. Writing assessments (see Rose *et al.* 2008) were conducted before and after two or three terms of classroom implementation. They are grouped in A–E grades used in Australian schools, in which a C grading is considered the acceptable standard. The chart compares growth rates of the top and bottom groups, and the gap between these groups before and after the programme. The top groups' growth, from C to A levels, is equivalent to over a year of expected growth. The bottom groups' growth from E to C levels is equivalent to three-years expected growth. The gap between them has almost halved.

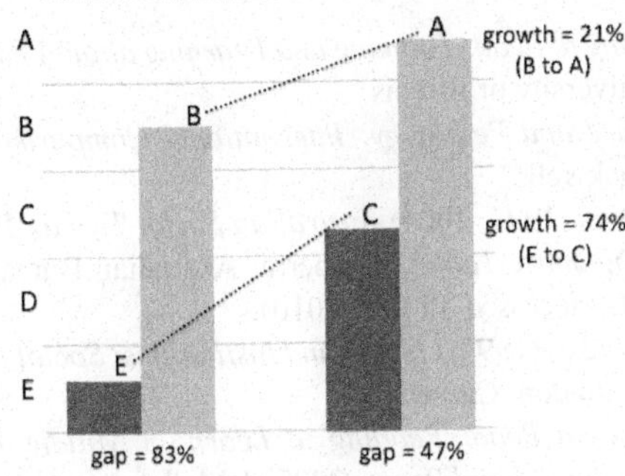

Figure 1. Averaged writing results 2008

Conclusion

Through the Reading to Learn programme, teachers are consistently showing that there is no need to accept the grossly unequal outcomes that have plagued education systems for so long, and disadvantaged so many children, particularly those from Indigenous backgrounds. Using the techniques outlined here, early years teachers are showing that there is no reason why all children cannot be independently reading, and successfully writing whole texts, within their first year of schooling, and so be thoroughly prepared for learning from reading in the years that follow. Likewise, upper primary and secondary teachers are showing that they can teach all their students the skills they need to learn the curriculum independently, at the same time as they are teaching that curriculum in the classroom.

The principle for making this possible is integration of the skills required for school learning, of both language and its contexts. Effective integration does not mean a hands-off approach that leaves children to try and construct their own learning. Rather it can only be built on systematic analysis of the nature of learning tasks in school, and careful design of teaching activities that will enable all students to achieve them. As these tasks always involve language, these analyses can only be built on a systematic understanding of the language task. With these tools it is possible to imagine an education system designed to serve a democratic society, with social equality as its guiding ideal.

References

Adams, M.J. (1990) *Beginning to Read: Thinking and Learning about Print: A Summary*. Urbana-Champaign: University of Illinois.

Alexander. R. (2000) *Culture and Pedagogy: International Comparisons in Primary Education*. London: Blackwell.

Australian Bureau of Statistics (1994, 2004) *Australian Social Trends 1994 and 2004: Education – National Summary Tables*. Canberra: Australian Bureau of Statistics. www.abs.gov.au/ausstats (accessed 30 June 2010).

Christie, F. and Martin, J.R. (eds.) (1997) *Genres and Institutions: Social Practices in the Workplace and School*. London: Cassell.

Culican, S. (2006) *Learning to Read: Reading to Learn: A Middle Years Literacy Intervention Research Project, Final Report 2003–4*. Melbourne: Catholic Education Office. www.readingtolearn.com.au (accessed 30 June 2010).

Folds, R. (1987) *Whitefella School: Education And Aboriginal Resistance*. Sydney: Allen & Unwin.

Gibbons, P. (2002) *Scaffolding Language, Scaffolding Learning*. Portsmouth, NH: Heinemann.

Gray, B., Rose, D. and Cowey, W. (1998) Project report for *Scaffolding Reading and Writing for Indigenous Children in School*, December 1998. Canberra: DEST Indigenous Education Branch and University of Canberra

Jabangardi-Poulson, C. (1988) The school curriculum I would like for my children. *Curriculum Perspectives* 8 (2): 68-69.

Lester, Y. (1993) *Yami: the autobiography of Yami Lester*. Alice Springs: Institute for Aboriginal Development.

McRae, D., Ainsworth, G., Cumming, J., Hughes, P., Mackay, T. Price, K., Rowland, M., Warhurst, J., Woods, D. and Zbar, V. (2000) *What has Worked, and Will Again: The IESIP Strategic Results Projects*. Canberra: Australian Curriculum Studies Association. www.readingtolearn.com.au (accessed 30 June 2010).

Malcolm, I. (1991) 'All right then, if you don't want to do that…': strategy and counter-strategy in classroom discourse management. *Guidelines* 13 (2): 11-17.

Martin, J.R. and Rose, D. (2007) *Working with Discourse: Meaning beyond the Clause*, 2nd edn. London: Continuum [2003].

Martin, J.R. and Rose, D. (2008) *Genre Relations: Mapping Culture*. London: Equinox.

Nassaji, H. and Wells, G. (2000) What's the use of 'triadic dialogue'?: an investigation of teacher-student interaction. *Applied Linguistics* 21 (3): 376-406.

Rose, D. (1992) Protection, self-determination and language learning in Aboriginal early childhood education: review of Aboriginal language education policy statements. *Education Australia*, Spring: 5-6.

Rose, D. (2004) Sequencing and pacing of the hidden curriculum: how indigenous children are left out of the chain. In J. Muller, A. Morais and B. Davies (eds.) *Reading Bernstein, Researching Bernstein*. London: RoutledgeFalmer, 91-107.

Rose, D. (2005) Democratising the classroom: a literacy pedagogy for the new generation. *Journal of Education* 37: 127-64. www.ukzn.ac.za/joe/joe_issues.htm (accessed 30 June 2010).

Rose, D. (2008) Writing as linguistic mastery: the development of genre-based literacy pedagogy. In D. Myhill, D. Beard, M. Nystrand and J. Riley (eds.) *Handbook of*

Writing Development. London: Sage, 151-66. www.readingtolearn.com.au (accessed 30 June 2010).

Rose, D., Gray, B. and Cowey, W. (1999) Scaffolding reading and writing for indigenous children in school. In P. Wignell (ed.) *Double Power: English Literacy and Indigenous Education*. Melbourne: National Language and Literacy Institute of Australia (NLLIA), 23-60.

Rose, D., Rose, M., Farrington, S and Page, S. (2008) Scaffolding literacy for indigenous health sciences students. *Journal of English for Academic Purposes* 7 (3): 166-80.

Williams, G. (1999) The pedagogic device and the production of pedagogic knowledge: a case example in early literacy education. In F. Christie (ed.) *Pedagogy and the Shaping of Consciousness: Linguistic and Social Processes*. London: Cassell, 88-122.

Notes

[1] **David Rose** is director of the international literacy programme Reading to Learn (www.readingtolearn.com.au) and an honorary associate of the Faculties of Arts at the University of Sydney. Reading to Learn trains teachers across all education sectors, but Dr Rose's work has been particularly concerned with Indigenous education in Australia. His research interests include literacy pedagogy and teacher education, and language and culture. He is the author of *The Western Desert Code* (Canberra: Pacific Linguistics, 2001), with J.R. Martin, *Working with Discourse: Meaning beyond the Clause* (London: Continuum, 2003, 2007) and also with J.R. Martin, *Genre Relations: Mapping Culture* (London: Equinox, 2008).

9 Enhancing literacy education for refugee children

Denise Lynch[1]

Introduction

According to the United Nations High Commission for Refugees (UNHCR) there were approximately 11.4 million refugees worldwide at the end of 2007, an increase of 2.4 million over the previous year (UNHCR 2008: 2). In the same period, a further estimated 740,000 individuals were waiting on a decision regarding their asylum claims. Children comprise a large proportion of these refugees fleeing situations of violence, terror and trauma. In Australia, for example, children constitute at least one third of the Australian refugee population, though precise figures are not always easy to establish (Australian Department of Immigration and Citizenship (DIAC) 2009a: 8).

Drawing primarily on Australian experience, but with wider relevance, this chapter discusses the needs of refugee children and youth, and it identifies the provision of literacy education as vital to the process of their coming to terms with life in their adopted country. Many excellent programmes for refugee children and youth may be found in schools and communities. However, in many cases, more needs to be done, while more consistently articulated policies should be framed, so that educational programmes specific to the needs and requirements of refugee children and youth are developed.

This chapter will briefly review the history of refugee settlement in Australia, before going on to identify the major groups of refugee children and youth who currently come to the country. It will then discuss the needs of each group, drawing attention to the legal, structural and political difficulties that can often impede the progress of refugee children and youth. In addition, the chapter will consider those educational programmes that offer positive learning experiences to refugee children. Finally, in the light of the discussion, it will conclude with some observations about the types of best practices that are needed for refugee children in the future.

A brief review of refugee settlement in Australia

Since white settlement in the late eighteenth century, Australia has had a long history of migration. Most early white settlers had been of Anglo-Celtic origins, though following the Second World War, Australia accepted migrants and refugees from Europe. Post-war groups included, for example, migrants and displaced persons from Italy, Greece and the former Yugoslavia. At this time these migrants and refugees contributed to the labour force, and were broadly acceptable within the White Australia Policy that had prevailed for some years.

Following changes brought about by the Whitlam Labor government (1972–75) there was a movement towards more integration of migrants, with less emphasis on assimilation than there had been in the past. This political movement was accompanied by legislation and policy that reflected a more multicultural Australia than before. Following Australia's contested involvement in the Vietnam War, there was a strong humanitarian push to assist the 'boat people' that came from Vietnam. In the following years the country accepted many migrants and refugees from Vietnam, Laos and Cambodia, and during the 1990s refugees were accepted from China. More recently Australia has also accepted refugees from African countries such as Sudan, Somalia, Ethiopia, and from Iraq and Afghanistan, among other countries.

This brief historical review of waves of acceptance gives an impression that migrants and refugees have had a positive transition to life in Australia. This is not always the case. Although Australia is a signatory to the 1951 Convention Relating to the Status of Refugees and the 1947 and 1989 United Nations Convention on the Rights of the Child (Refugee Council of Australia 2009a: 1), there is at times a level of subtle and not so subtle racism that often emerges more strongly in times of economic difficulty. This has often influenced policy making and service provision for refugee children. Tascon writes:

> Australia … is deeply inscribed with racialised-exclusions and the need to determine who crosses the borders. It is a need that attempts to protect its whiteness. There are ethnic/religious dimensions to this whiteness including the preservation of Anglo-Celtic and Judeo-Christian traditions (Tascon 2002: 3).

While blatant expressions of racism have been deplored in Australia, the race factor has continued to be linked with policies and practices around refugees and migration. Consider, for example, the Tampa Incident (of August 2001) when asylum seekers on a refugee boat were wrongly accused of throwing their children overboard. This claim was essentially accepted by many Australians until it was disproved (Mares 2002; Manne 2004; Christie and Sidhu 2006).

From the mid-1990s on, there has been a stronger emphasis on 'skilled migration' than in the past, and a more penalising approach to refugees who have not come to Australia through the official channels. In some ways children of asylum seekers and refugees often became the collateral damage of the 'policies of deterrence' of the Howard federal government (1995–2007). Although there was some public disquiet about the treatment of refugee children in Australia, they were removed from mandatory detention only after 2005. In addition, the mandatory detention of adults arriving in Australia without proper documentation has continued to the present time.

The groups of refugee children and youth

Refugee children and youth are not a homogenous group, for their histories and previous life experiences reveal significant differences. Such children differ, within both the international and Australian contexts, and as they arrive in their adopted countries with varying familial, social and educational backgrounds. Regardless of background, all refugee children arrive in their host country without making a choice to be there. They mostly have been subject to trauma and violence, some having have had a range of life and death experiences that can have lifelong consequences.

Depending on their circumstances, children and youth arrive in their host country with the legal status of either 'refugee' or 'asylum seeker'. Their legal status affects their entitlements and their access to services, including health services. Their status also affects their sense of identity and their sense of belonging in their new country. Within the broad cohort of asylum seekers and refugees, the following groups can be found:

- School-age children who are refugees, or living in refugee-like situations (e.g. displaced persons or asylum seekers or the children of asylum seekers). Within this group there are some who have come from countries where they have no history of any formal schooling and some who have had an experience of school that is similar to the host country.
- Young people who are chronologically and legally no longer children, and because of their age and/or previous history are not able to access mainstream school education (Pittman, Herbert, Land and O'Neill 2004; Brophy and Page 2007; Woods 2009).
- Unaccompanied children and young people who arrive in the host country without family or close ties of any kind. There is a Memorandum of Understanding between the Australian government and the various states, by which these children are placed in foster care under the responsibility of the relevant state welfare department (Crock 2007).

- Children with an experience of mandatory detention or detention-like quality of life. Mandatory detention for children was discontinued in Australia in 2005, and children are often placed in foster care in the local area of the detention centre, while their parents are still detained in one of the detention facilities in Australia, or 'offshore'.

The above groups suggest something of the different experiences of refugee children and young adults, especially as they present in Australia. They also suggest something of the ways that some children and their families experience disadvantage, through the structural and legal limitations associated with their status in their new country. Children who have a permanent refugee status, for example, cannot be deported, though others may be subject to deportation if their legal status changes.

The manner in which a society treats refugee children and their well-being reflects how that society identifies, and addresses, those groups deemed worthy of inclusion or exclusion. Judgements about who 'belongs' in the host country and who has the right to 'enter and stay' are thus often contested. In the contemporary world, when so many refugees and their children are to be found, the issue of how they are treated has become a matter of social justice. In the broadest political sense, the issue concerns the rights and responsibilities of citizenship, entitlement and belonging.

In Australia, refugee children are often not specified and represented in official figures, except in specialised reports and documents. They are often included with adults or parents in statistical data, and except when they are unaccompanied, they are not clearly visible within migration and refugee statistics (see Australian Department of Immigration and Citizenship (DIAC) 2008 and Refugee Council of Australia 2009b). Polzer and Hammond argue that refugee and asylum-seeker populations are often made invisible to suit the political requirements of a government and nation. They state:

> Invisibility is a relationship between those who have the power to see or to choose not to see, and, on the other hand, those who lack the power to demand to be seen or to protect themselves from the negative effects of imposed visibility … Politicised refugee groups and refugee advocates aim to increase their visibility to powerful institutions whom they see as potential allies in order to increase their access to resources and legitimacy. Often, however, powerful institutions such as the state aim to impose categorizations and labels which are against the interests of individuals. From this perspective, visibility equals being controlled, and even those who choose invisibility for themselves are disempowered, for they use their invisibility as a protective shield when true legal, political and social protection is not forthcoming (Polzer and Hammond 2008: 419).

This view is supported by professionals and academics (see Winston-Smith 2008; Sidhu and Taylor 2007; Christie and Sidhu 2002, 2006). Why is the issue of official recognition important to refugee children? It is because of the relative 'invisibility' of refugee children in Australia that federal and state policies for dealing with their needs have often been produced in piecemeal fashion at best, though at times there has been no clearly apparent policy at all. In order to improve the situation the children must first 'appear' in the political and policy debates in the educational community and the broader society.

Despite the limitations of federal policies, the states – which are primarily responsible for educational policy under the Australian constitution – have developed many effective programmes. The Department of Education and Training in the state of NSW has recently developed a raft of excellent programmes to support teachers working with refugee children in schools. It also has policies covering multicultural education, ESL acquisition, literacy and anti-racism. These resources can be found through the DET website https://www.det.nsw.edu.au

The needs of refugee children

While refugees arrive where they seem reasonably safe, their well-being and their children's well-being are not guaranteed, and their adjustment and integration into the new environment are often difficult. The major needs of refugee children are related to good health, including mental health and provision of employment for their parents, appropriate housing and appropriate education (particularly English language education). All these are essential in contributing to a sense of positive well-being for the children and their families. A positive sense of well-being is very strongly linked with identity and a feeling of belonging, and this can be linked to achieving a resolution of a sense of loss associated with separation from the country of origin.

Health and welfare

The health needs of refugee children have been documented clearly in the literature. Many children have not received vaccinations or dental and eye checks in their own countries, and they thus need urgent attention to those matters after their arrival in Australia (Lynch and Cunninghame 2000).

In respect of their psychological and emotional well-being, some children have witnessed the death of relatives, and have led generally disrupted lives, leading, among other things, to little or no schooling. Even where children arrive with parents in an accepting host country, it is likely that they are suffering grief and loss for what they have left behind, leading to depression and other mental health problems. The psychological problems are various, though their expression often reflects the cultural values of the ethnic groups from which the children come. A study undertaken in the UK of Somali families and their use of religious beliefs to deal with stress indicates this (Whittaker *et al.* 2005). Eisenbruch's work on 'cultural bereavement' has relevance here, as it emphasises individuals' cultural interpretation of their situation and ways of dealing with it. He states:

> A comprehensive approach to the diagnosis of refugee mental health must be culturally relevant, assume nothing about distress versus disorder and allow for the patient's cultural constructions of mental health (Eisenbruch, 1991: 678).

The ability to move forward and resolve grief is determined in part by the collaborative programmes available to the child in the host country. However, Eisenbruch and others stress that it is important that refugee children are not pathologised so that they are encouraged to understand that grief is part of life's experiences and that it does not have to be a permanent part of their lives. It is important, in other words, that refugee children are not automatically labelled with a mental illness and that their school is seen as a place of normality (Guerin *et al.* 2004). This consideration has consequences for the nature of their educational experience including their literacy programmes, which need to be constructive and supportive in character.

Two major factors that contribute to the health and well-being of refugee children after their arrival, alluded to already above, are the provision of work for their parents, and appropriate accommodation for the family. In fact, parental employment and provision of safe housing both contribute to a developing sense of well-being in children, assisting emergence of a positive sense of identity and of belonging in the host country, while they also assist in dealing with grief. None of these issues can be separated from each other, for they all impact on refugee children's ability to adjust, contributing in turn to their capacity to achieve educationally. Guerin *et al.* (2004), for example, found a positive relationship between English ability and physical health in a study of Somali refugees in New Zealand.

Educational needs

Educationally, when refugee children arrive in their new country they have a range of needs that often include the need to learn English, the need to enter mainstream schooling, the need to learn to function in school environments (some have known no schooling in their own countries) and to adopt appropriate school behaviours. The quality of the initiation period of children and young people sets an important foundation for their future lives in the host country. Children can begin a new part of their lives that gives them hope, acquisition of a language and the sense of being able to 'fit into' their new world.

The value of a welcoming school is sometimes underestimated, but teaching personnel and social workers consistently refer to the positive influence of an authentic hospitable school, regarding it as a foundational anchor for new students and their families. Hoddinott, principal of a secondary school with a high refugee intake in Sydney, refers to the importance of the school's 'ethical connections' with students and their families, and to the teaching of what she calls 'cultural literacy', which is, she says, 'essential for understanding both the school curriculum and Australian society'. Equally, the school seeks to respect the cultural values and expectations of the children (Hoddinott, 2006; see also New South Wales Department of Education and Training 2004).

In regard to the provision of programmes in English language and literacy in Australia, the general practice for all secondary migrant children for some time has been to place them initially in intensive language programmes, while primary aged children enrol in their own age schools. Secondary arrivals, including refugee children, are enrolled for up to four school terms in one of several intensive language programmes in urban areas. In these, the object is to establish a degree of proficiency in oral and written language before the children are moved into mainstream classes, where they may continue to receive specialist assistance, depending on resources and locality. The English programmes initially teach basic skills in phonics, spelling and reading, giving attention to development of reading fluency and comprehension, as well as skill in writing. The full range of Key Learning Areas of the NSW Board of Studies is also taught in English, while associated skills are developed in uses of IT.

In time, and with growing proficiency, refugee children are assisted, like their 'mainstream' classmates, to develop a sense of the multiple literacies of the contemporary world, coming to understand that literacy activities are social practices (Harste 2003: 8), and that as such they represent ways of making meaning. All this helps build a sense of the ways of making meaning found in a contemporary English-speaking culture, while allowing reflection on the ways of meaning making found in the refugee children's own language and culture. For example, if children come from a country where they have witnessed violence and their families have barely escaped with their lives, they need help in accommodating this experience while also gaining new knowledge as part of the school curriculum.

One initiative is reported by Rousseau *et al.* concerning engagement of refugee children in creative writing workshops in Canada. The refugee children engaged in creative expression workshops, using their newly acquired language to 'participate in the construction of a meaningful personal world while simultaneously strengthening the link of the child to the group' (Rousseau *et al.* 2005).

An important factor known to assist children in the school environment is the involvement of families in the school community. A welcoming school is desirable for all families, but it is particularly helpful to refugee populations, among whom English acquisition has been difficult for parents who are not in the work force or actively involved in the community. For example, there is a school-based programme in Sydney, which is an art programme for refugee mothers. Exhibitions are organised as part of the programme and this collaborative work has had positive outcomes for children and their families. In other areas of Sydney, mothers are invited to visit the schools for social events, and efforts are made to draw them into school life.

Overall, for refugee children entering mainstream schools the policies and practices need to demonstrate how the children can be 'included', can be safe, can be optimistic about their future and become literate and knowing in their new language. Under these conditions, the literacy acquisition of the refugee child is truly enhanced as the 'whole' child actively participates in this process. The role of teachers, counsellors and ethnic community models cannot be underestimated. These people often represent the first bridge of trust for a child with a refugee background. Bishop states:

> Teachers seek to create sociocultural contexts wherein learning takes place actively, reflectively, and where learners can not only use a variety of learning styles, but also have the power to determine which learning styles they need to use. In other words, creating contexts where they can safely bring what they know and who they are into the learning relationship (Bishop 2003: 229).

The needs of older children and young people without a history of any formal education

Older children and youth often arrive in their host country after a protracted period spent in reaching their destination. In these circumstances young people have often experienced unstable or disrupted schooling and sometimes no schooling at all. Their chances of experiencing a positive school environment in their new country are diminished. Recent examples of such young people and their problems have included arrivals from Sudan to the UK and Western Europe, and Australia, and Central American arrivals from Guatemala and Santo Domingo to the US. These children, if they are younger than 16 years, often bring little awareness of, or capacity to be, a 'school child' or be part of a school community. They wish to learn, but they have great difficulty, partly because they have had little experience of understanding their role as a student in the school community. Guerin *et al.* (2004: 18) report an example of Somali children in New Zealand, who, though strongly influenced by their own family, religion and community, were not much affected by school expectations in their new country. For these students, the opportunity to gain an education was reduced, and it had a diminished impact on them.

Apart from problems with schooling, many older children suffer from other problems of adjustment. They may have managed homes and cared for others under shocking conditions in their country of origin, and they may still be managing households in their new country. They often need to enter a school where their academic group is much younger and, for the purposes of schooling at least, they have to reframe their lives as 'dependent' persons. For older refugee children it is often very hard to retain a sense of dignity in these circumstances. These experiences often leave young people with reduced self esteem, a sense of little academic achievement and an increased sense of their own exclusion (Cassity and Gow 2005; Candappa and Igbinigie 2003). A study by Poppit and Fray (2007) examined sources of stress for Sudanese adolescent refugees. They concluded that such young people needed considerable support in moving between the cultural values of their own people and those of the new culture, and that they often required assistance with what they felt to be new gender roles, as well as competence in English.

For the young people aged 16–25 years, who have had little formal education, their ability to access appropriate programmes other than language classes often poses difficulty. They often find menial jobs, with low pay, live in poor accommodation and have very little optimism about their host country. Such young people often receive ongoing assistance from various charitable agencies that try to help them develop greater self-esteem, as well as acquiring greater skills.

To address difficulties of adjustment and poor self-esteem among the young in other ways, a number of programmes have been developed in Australia and elsewhere to help refugee youth come to terms with their new culture, while also retaining aspects of their past. One such programme in Canada (Carranza 2007) involved mothers from El Salvador, who engaged in teaching their adolescent daughters about the positive aspects of their background. The author speaks of the mothers being actively involved in their daughters' development and giving them protection and self-esteem in order to move successfully into their new culture, though keeping their Salvadorian history and culture (see also Olliff 2007, who describes the use of sport for refugee youth in Australia).

Unaccompanied children and young people

One known factor that has a decisive impact on the resilience of refugee children and youth in dealing with hardship is family support. Hence it is unaccompanied children who are amongst the most vulnerable of all refugees. When families are separated, or children have different visa provisions from their parents, or they are alone for whatever reasons, the difficulties for them are increased. In the UK, where there are 5,000 unaccompanied asylum-seeking young people, it is reported that there are often grave concerns for their well-being and future (Kohli 2007; Veale *et al.* 2003). Crock studied 85 of the 290 unaccompanied children who arrived in Australia seeking asylum between 1999 and 2003. She identified the need for particular programmes that addressed literacy education, counselling and psychiatric care, as well as mentoring into both skilled and unskilled occupations. She wrote of the importance of securing an alternative family for the unaccompanied refugee and the relevance of a supportive community. As a lawyer, she also stressed the need for legal systems that address the particular requirements of asylum-seeking children who are travelling alone, thereby achieving their full protection in law (Crock 2007).

Children with an experience of mandatory detention

In Australia, where children or their parents have a history of detention, they have a very negative experience of life in the host country. As stated earlier, since 2005, children are no longer kept in mandatory detention. However, some have had detention-like experiences before they were able to achieve 'refugee' status, enabling them to live in the Australian community. According to DIAC,

> [a]s at 3 July 2009, there were 101 children (aged under 18 years) in immigration detention. 25 were detained in the community under residence determinations, 69 were in alternative temporary detention in the community and seven were in immigration residential housing (Australian Department of Immigration and Citizenship (DIAC) 2009b: 4).

If refugee status has not been achieved for asylum-seeking children and/or their families, they suffer a very precarious experience, as their legal position is unsure and the provision of services to them is minimal (Lynch 2008). Since it is known that the primary need of refugee children is to develop a sense of identity and well-being in the new country, it is clear that an experience of detention works against this development. There is a raft of studies in Australia and other countries that detail the negative effects of detention on children (e.g. Sultan and O'Sullivan 2001; Cemlyn and Briskman 2003). Even though children are no longer held in detention centres, mandatory detention for their parents and other adults in their families still has a negative impact on the children themselves. Refugee children in these circumstances are very vulnerable, and they need constant support and advice during the often lengthy periods of time taken while their parents' applications for acceptance as refugees are processed.

Within the situations discussed above in different groups of refugee children, it is important to be cognisant of the resilience and capacity of all children in the challenging worlds they meet as refugees. While being young makes them vulnerable, this can also make them inventive, creative and positive in situations of extreme difficulty. These children, if supported appropriately, have a history of survival that is part of their identity as much as the past trauma is also a part of their identity. Many children find connections, friendships and an ability to learn in different ways through times of transition. Many do achieve very adequate adjustments to life in their schools, and they go on to make good contributions to their new community, often attracting significant community support to help them. Hoddinott, for example, the school principal mentioned above, established a trust fund in 2008 to assist a gifted refugee student to stay at school so that she could go on to enter university. Other refugee students, though sometimes perceived as unsuccessful in school environments, often do achieve in many ways, belonging to homes and communities where they are recognised as successful and productive (Bottrell 2007).

Best policy and practice

Overall, a summary of the important principles that can enhance literacy in refugee children is as follows:

- Refugee children and youth should be recognised in policy as a distinct group of children and young adults with particular educational needs.
- School programmes need consistently and sensitively to address all the needs of refugee children, intellectual, emotional and social, taking into account their varied pasts.
- Literacy programmes are most successful when designed to fit the particular learning needs of refugee children and youth. There should be no policy of 'one programme fits all'.
- Literacy and other educational programmes are needed for those older children and youth who do not fit into mainstream school environments.
- A 'strengths-based' perspective should be adopted that balances any negative conditions experienced by children with the resilience they find within their home and community.
- Unaccompanied children and children with detention experiences need to be given appropriate counselling and support, recognising their cultural survival strategies while also acknowledging the negative consequences of labels to do with mental illness.

Conclusion

The educational needs of refugee children and youth cover a much greater range of issues than acquisition of English, important though that is. Good educational programmes will acknowledge and address the range of needs, personal, emotional and social, that refugee children and youth experience. Literacy acquisition is strongly linked to the development of children's personal identities in their adopted countries. Development of proficiency in English literacy must be understood as one significant dimension of the overall programmes offered to refugee children and youth, because it facilitates their entry to their new country. The best and most effective educational programmes acknowledge the backgrounds of the refugees, working in constructive ways to help them build a positive sense of their futures. We have such a responsibility to refugee children and youth, while we also have the ability to be active in promoting their progress, bringing positive rewards both to the children and to the societies they have joined.

References

Australian Department of Immigration and Citizenship (DIAC) (2008) Fact Sheet 60. Produced by the National Communications Branch, Department of Immigration and Citizenship, Canberra.   Revised 25 August 2008. http://www.immi.gov.au/media/fact-sheets/60refugee.htm

Australian Department of Immigration and Citizenship (DIAC) (2009a) Refugee and Humanitarian Issues, Australia's Response. June, 2009. http://www.immi.gov.au/media/publications/refugee/ref-hum-issues/pdf/refugee-humanitarian-issues-june09.pdf (accessed 1 August 2009).

Australian Department of Immigration and Citizenship (DIAC) (2009b) Immigration Detention Statistics Summary, Community and Detention Services Division, DIAC, as at 8 July 2009. http://www.immi.gov.au/managing-australias-borders/detention/_pdf/immigration-detention-statistics-20090703.pdf (accessed 1 August 2009).

Bishop, R. (2003) Changing power relations in education: Kaupapa Ma'ri messages for 'mainstream' education in Aotearoa/New Zealand, (1). *Comparative Education* 39 (2): 221-38.

Bottrell, D. (2007) Resistance, resilience and social identities: reframing problem youth and the problem of schooling. *Journal of Youth Studies* 10 (5): 597-61.

Brophy, M. and Page, E. (2007) Radio literacy and life skills for out-of-school youth in Somalia. *Journal of International Cooperation in Education* 10 (1): 135-47.

Candappa, M. and Igbinigie, I. (2003) Everyday worlds of young refugees in London. *Feminist Review* 73 (1): 54-65.

Carranza, M.E. (2007) Building resilience and resistance against racism and discrimination among Salvadorian female youth in Canada. *Child and Family Social Work* 4 (12): 1-9. http://www.blackwell-synergy.com/doi/full/10.1111/j.1365-2206 (accessed 10 July 2007).

Cassity, E. and Gow, G. (2005) Making up for lost time: the experiences of Southern Sudanese young refugees in high schools, (Programs and Practice). *Youth Studies, Australia* 24 (3): 51-55.

Cemlyn, S. and Briskman, L. (2003) Asylum, children's rights and social work. *Child and Family Social Work* 8: 163-78.

Christie, P. and Sidhu, R. (2002) Responding to globalisation: refugees and the challenges facing Australian schools. *Mots Pluriels* 21 (May): 11. http://www.arts.uwa.edu.au/MotsPluriels/MP2102pcrs.html (accessed 6 February 2009).

Christie, P. and Sidhu, R. (2006) Governmentality and fearless speech: framing the education of asylum seeker and refugee children in Australia *Oxford Review of Education* 32 (4): 449-65.

Crock, M. (2007) *Seeking Asylum Alone: A Comparative Study of Laws, Policy and Practice in Australia, UK and US*. Sydney: Themis Press.

Eisenbruch, M. (1991) From post-traumatic stress disorder to cultural bereavement: diagnosis of South East Asian refugees. *Social Science and Medicine* 33 (6): 673-80.

Guerin, B., Guerin, P., Diiriye, R.O. and Abdi, A. (2004) Living in a close community: the everyday life of Somali refugees. *Journal of the Australian College Community*, 1-34. http://www.waikato.ac.nz/migration/docs/guerin-sent-network-paper.pdf (accessed 20 March 2009).

Harste, J.C. (2003) What do we mean by literacy now? *Voices from the Middle* 10 (3) (March): 8-12.

Hoddinott, D. (2006) Cultural and linguistic diversity: issues for schools. A paper given at the Conference on Students with Additional Learning Needs: Theory, Practice and Intervention – what works?, organised by the Children's Hospital Education Research Institute, Sydney, 7–8 September 2006. http://www.cheri.com.au/PDF_Files /CHERI%20XI%20Conf%202006/print%20version/PVHoddinottDorothy.pdf (accessed 20 August 2009).

Kohli, R.K.S. (2007) *Social Work with Unaccompanied Asylum Seeking Children*. Basingstoke: Palgrave Macmillan.

Lynch, D. (2008) Violence and the state: asylum seeker children. In B. Fawcett and F. Waugh (eds.) *Addressing Violence, Abuse and Oppression: Debates and Challenges*. London: Routledge, 122-32.

Lynch, M. and Cunninghame, C. (2000) Understanding the needs of young asylum seekers. *Archives of Disease in Childhood* 83: 384-87.

Manne, R. (2004) Sending them home: refugees and the new politics of indifference. *Quarterly Essay* 13: 1-95. http://search.informit.com.au/documentSummary;dn= 706300815726494;res=IELHSS ISSN: 1832-0953 (accessed 20 August 2009).

Mares, P. (2002) *Borderline: Australia's Response to Refugees and Asylum Seekers in the Wake of the Tampa*. Sydney: University of New South Wales Press.

New South Wales Department of Education and Training (2004) *Ethnic Affairs Priorities Statement*. Sydney: New South Wales Department of Education. https://www.det.nsw .edu.au/media/downloads/reports_stats/eaps_report/eapsreport2004.pdf (accessed 28 August 2009).

Olliff, L. (2007) Playing for the future: the role of sport and recreation in supporting refugee young people to 'settle well' in Australia. *Youth Studies Australia* 27 (1): 52-60.

Pittman, S., Herbert, T., Land, C. and O'Neill, C. (2004) *Profile of Young Australians: Facts, Figures and Issues*. Melbourne: Foundation for Young Australians.

Polzer, T. and Hammond, L. (2008) Invisible displacement. *Journal of Refugee Studies* 21 (4): 417-31.

Poppit, G. and Fray, R. (2007) Sudanese adolescent refugees: acculturation and acculturative stress. *Australian Journal of Guidance and Counselling*,17 (2): 160-81.

Refugee Council of Australia (2009a) *Australia's Refugee Program*. http://www.refugeecouncil.org.au/arp/faqs.html (accessed 25 July 2009).

Refugee Council of Australia (2009b) *Australia's Refugee Program, Australian Statistics*. http://www.refugeecouncil.org.au/arp/stats-02.html (accessed 9 March 2009).

Rousseau, C., Drapeau, A., Lacroix, L., Deogratias, B. and Heusch, N. (2005) Evaluation of a classroom project of creative expression workshops for refugee and immigrant children. *Journal of Child Psychology and Psychiatry* 46 (2): 180-85.

Sidhu, R. and Taylor, S.C. (2007) Educational provision for refugee youth in Australia: left to chance? *Journal of Sociology* 43 (3): 283-300.

Sultan, A. and O'Sullivan, K. (2001) Psychological disturbances in asylum seekers held in long term detention: a participant-observer account. *Medical Journal of Australia* 175: 593-96.

Tascon, S. (2002) Refugees and asylum seekers in Australia: border crossers of the post colonial imaginary. *Mots Pluriels* 21 (May). http://motspluriels.arts.uwa.edu.au /MP2102smt.html (accessed 13 May 2009).

UNHCR (2008) *United Nations High Commissioner for Refugees, 2007 Global Trends: Refugees, Asylum Seekers, Returnees, Internally Displaced Person and Stateless Persons*. http://www.unhcr.org/statistics/STATISTICS/4852366f2.pdf (accessed 11 September 2008).

Veale, A., Palaudaries, L. and Gibbons, C. (2003) *Separated Children Seeking Asylum in Ireland*. Dublin: The Irish Refugee Council.

Whittaker, S., Hardy, G., Lewis, K. and Buchan, L. (2005) An exploration of the psychological well-being with young Somali refugee and asylum seeker women. *Clinical Child Psychology and Psychiatry* 10 (2): 177-96.

Winston-Smith, J. (2008) Pathways to children's settlement, the Brotherhood's outreach model of intervention for young refugee children and their families. http://www.bsl.org .au/pdfs/In_their_own_right_forum_JanetWSpresentation_18July2008.pdf (accessed 10 March 2009).

Woods, A. (2009) Learning to be literate: issues of pedagogy for recently arrived refugee youth in Australia. *Critical Inquiry in Language Studies* 6 (1 and 2) (January): 81-101.

Notes

[1]   **Denise Lynch** is senior lecturer at the University of Sydney in Social Work and Policy Studies, Faculty of Education and Social Work. Her professional experience is with child protection and violence, and families in government and non-government sectors. Her research interests include asylum-seeking children in Australia, child protection, child neglect and international child welfare. Publications include: 'Violence and the state, asylum seeker children', in B. Fawcett and F. Waugh (eds.), *Addressing Violence, Abuse and Oppression, Debates and Challenges* (London: Routledge, 2008); and 'Cultural diversity in practice: working with migrants and refugees', in A. Ohara and Z. Weber (eds.), *Skills for Human Service Practice* (Melbourne: Oxford University Press, 2006).

10 Envoi

Frances Christie and Alyson Simpson[1]

Introduction

We began this volume with the suggestion that language and literacy educators and professional social workers might usefully discuss the importance of literacy in the modern world and the responsibilities of the community in ensuring provision of literacy education, especially for the many disadvantaged. There are of course many reasons for teaching literacy apart from those to do with averting social disadvantage: literacy is an important resource in personal development, allowing access to the pleasures of reading and to the confidence and independence that can come from being able to write for oneself. Language and literacy educators tend to stress the importance of literacy in these terms, while social workers, in so far as they think about literacy at all, inevitably reflect on the negative effects for those who do not have adequate literacy. Chris Riley (chapter 7), for example, initiated his Youth Off The Streets programme to address the personal and social problems of youth who would otherwise 'fall through the cracks', sometimes even ending up in jail. He aims with his colleagues to teach them skills, including literacy skills, that will enable them to overcome disadvantage. In general, social workers tend to see literacy in terms of remediation and overcoming hardships, for they see at first hand how seriously disadvantaged are those who lack literacy. Language and literacy educators, on the other hand, tend to view teaching literacy more in terms of promoting the personal and intellectual development of those whom they teach, while they also recognise the problems faced by children who do not learn literacy adequately. Overall, the two professional communities operate with different priorities, and they do not always enter into each other's point of view, though their broad general concerns can overlap.

In what senses then, can the deliberations of each community of professionals inform each other? If advocacy is built on strong partnerships that create good relationships with students, then what can we gain from a dialogue between the two professions? In this final chapter we propose to identify some issues that run through the chapters we have assembled, about which we have a large measure of agreement.

Early intervention and the teaching of literacy

The seriously disadvantaged members of the community typically reveal poor literacy skills, though early intervention can make a difference (Vinson, chapter 6). In the Australian state of New South Wales, for example, 60 per cent of prison inmates have been said to be 'not functionally literate or numerate' and do not achieve even a year 10 education (New South Wales Legislative Council 2001: 20). According to the NSW Director of Public Prosecutions, Cowdery (2006: 3), 'functional illiteracy' in prison inmates is very high. This, he has said, reflects a trend found elsewhere in Australia and other parts of the world. Though, as we noted in chapter 1, there is no easy cause-and-effect relationship between low literacy levels and social disadvantage, the two are at least correlated. Moreover, literacy capacity cannot readily be separated from other life skills, a fact recognised in several intervention programmes to which Cowdery alluded, in the USA and Canada, which focused on intervening among disadvantaged children and their families, aiming to develop habits of co-operation in working with others in school, of identifying goals for learning and of developing generally socially rewarded behaviours, where these included achieving literate skills. It seems clear that successful early intervention programmes can lead to much enhanced life skills. In one study of a group of students in an early intervention programme in the USA, the students were traced till they had reached the age of 27. Relatively few had had any criminal record, compared with a similar group who had not undergone such a programme; moreover, they had achieved reasonable educations (some including college graduation), and compared with those not involved in the intervention, they 'had significantly higher earnings and were more likely to own a home' (Cowdery 2006: 6). The evidence overall suggests that where efforts are made to achieve very early intervention in the development and education of children in socially deprived circumstances, the effects of hardships can be turned around.

These matters noted, very good evidence also exists to show that literacy performance must be sustained and promoted over the years of schooling, for there is at times a misleading view that literacy learning is primarily a function of the early years, and that, the foundations being laid, beyond that literacy learning will progress reasonably easily. Rose (chapter 8) has noted the tendency often found in schools for the practice of giving specific attention to teaching reading to fall away after the early years. Similarly, overt teaching about writing – its different text types and their social purposes – often falls away as well, especially by the early secondary years.

Literacy in the middle years

Many children struggle through the years of a primary education, not really coping with their literacy learning, though their problems may not appear very visible until they reach the secondary school, when their inadequate literacy becomes acute. It is in the so-called 'middle years' of upper primary and junior secondary school that poor literacy performance often becomes most obvious, for this is when children must cope with the increasingly specialist language of the different school subjects that are a feature of secondary schooling. Several studies in different parts of the world point to the difficulties of students in early adolescence and in junior secondary school, some of them already alluded to by Christie (chapter 2). In England, for example, a two-year pilot study (2003–2005) conducted in the light of a government Green Paper, sought to address problems with school performance among 11–14-year-old students, and this led to a new programme, Assessing Pupils' Progress, or APP for Key Stages 3 and 4 (Qualifications and Curriculum Authority 2009), providing guidelines for teaching reading and writing in the junior secondary years. Fang and Schleppegrell (2008: 1-17) offer a recent discussion of developments in the USA, focusing in particular on the teaching of reading in the content areas in secondary school, while Christie and Derewianka (2008) discuss writing development over all the years of schooling, including the transition years from upper primary to secondary school. Literate language changes as students move from childhood to adolescence, though the linguistic patterns involved are often not well understood by teachers, who need considerable knowledge themselves in order to guide their students' learning of literacy, through adolescence, and on to adult life.

Literacy as multimodal awareness

The word 'literacy' – as distinct from reading and writing – dates from the twentieth century (Christie, chapter 2), so that historically it is a very recent term. One of the achievements of much educational theory and practice in the twentieth century was that the term came into increasingly common usage, serving to unify the activities of reading and writing, for they have been too often understood as discrete, independent skills. As originally conceived, literacy was of course associated with print materials, where these might involve some accompanying illustrations or even diagrams. A further achievement of the early twenty-first century is the growing acceptance and recognition of the phenomenon which is multiliteracy (Simpson and Walsh, chapter 3), referring to the range of multimodal resources with which in the modern world we shape and communicate knowledge and information of many kinds, verbal, visual and verbal/visual.

Studies have shown that learning to cope with multiple modes of communication encourages children to develop a metaconsciousness about creating meaning that supports their literacy development across a range of curriculum areas within demanding education contexts. Van Leeuwen's study of primary school children visiting the London Science Museum (2000), for example, showcases how children are stimulated to design multimodal texts to communicate their learning in response to a non-traditional environment. Unsworth and colleagues' study of material in high-stakes literacy tests in the state of NSW (Unsworth, Thomas and Bush 2004) demonstrates the increasing need for students to combine information from complementary semiotic resources in order to successfully comprehend multimodal texts. Reflecting on this inter-semiotic complexity within interactive game situations leads Gee to write:

> The learner needs to learn not only how to understand and produce meanings in a particular semiotic domain that are recognizable to those affiliated with the domain, but, in addition, how to think about the domain at a 'meta' level as a complex system of interrelated parts (Gee 2003: 23).

As children are challenged to read more and more complex texts, it is vital that they be supported to develop multiliterate skills and awareness.

Literacy and imaginative activity

Among the many reasons for teaching literacy must be its capacity to open doors to the imaginative pleasures of literature and of drama (Ewing, chapter 5), while active exploration of both necessarily facilitates constructive talk, a matter also suggested by Riley and Randall (chapter 7) discussing the experience of disadvantaged youth working on texts for young readers. For example, a study of the use of drama-related strategies with underprivileged students shows the importance of substantive conversation as a means of creating links between everyday life and literary texts to improve social and educational meta-awareness (Hertzberg, Foor and Manga 2006). The importance of literature and of the imaginative experiences that can be achieved in exploratory talk about it are emphasised in the Cambridge Primary Review, chaired by Alexander (2009: 269)

In a study of children's reading choices (Simpson 2008), authors, illustrators and school students aged 7 to 13 years of age were interviewed for their opinions on the value of literary texts. All participants spoke of the importance of reading for enjoyment as well as critical thinking. The results show that the current focus on testing regimes and literacy skills works against building future patterns of lifelong engagement with reading. As Lewis, who writes about learning through storying, states:

> With more and continued emphasis on literacy standards and measuring and testing of specific skills deemed important to reading development are we in fact neglecting the imaginative and creative importance of literacy? Are we contributing to the decline of children reading for pleasure, enjoyment, imaginative exploration and discovery? (Lewis 2007: 66).

Michael Rosen, British Children's Laureate (2007–2009), pleads for the opportunity to give children reading experiences that 'intrigue, entertain, educate, amuse, excite, stir up and challenge' (Rosen 2005:14). It is clear that these kinds of opportunities will be available within creative and imaginative learning contexts.

Literacy and social responsibility

A century ago many people in English-speaking countries had little or no literacy, yet they were able to achieve gainful employment. Even a generation ago, many had limited literacy skills at best, though they nonetheless often found paid employment. In the early twenty-first century, however, to be literate is to be possessed of one of the essential skills required for effective participation in modern life, and its absence seriously impedes capacity to find rewarding employment. But apart from the utilitarian values associated with mastery of literacy, there are the many other values to do with personal enrichment and capacity to function independently, discussed for example by Lynch (chapter 9) with respect to refugee children, though quite fundamentally involved in the discussions in all the other chapters in this book.

Our discussions with social workers and teachers have highlighted the shared professional concerns that both groups have to improve the learning and living circumstances of all students. Yet it is also clear that there are at times gaps in the conversation due to a lack of shared understanding between social workers and teachers. Because of the rather different preoccupations of the two professions, it is rare for either discipline to gain good insight into the other's knowledge base and core practices, though the two groups work with those who often need both literacy programmes and social intervention. The case study of Youth Off The Streets, for example, successfully models a practical operation that blends the combined powers of social workers and teachers to give the best possible outcomes for students. As Mrs Lou Single, Deputy Director of Education Services of Youth Off The Streets and Principal of the EDEN Learning Centre, argues, it is vital that an appropriate sense of educational principles underpins a welfare approach to helping young people. In the interest of social justice, there is an important need to set up strong pathways of communication between social workers and teachers, ensuring effective literacy teaching in the future.

References

Alexander, R. (ed.) (2009) *Children, their World, their Education: Final Report and Recommendations of the Cambridge Primary Review*. London and New York: Routledge.

Christie, F. and Derewianka, B. (2008) *School Discourse: Learning to Write across the Years of Schooling*. Continuum Discourse Series. London and New York: Continuum.

Cowdery, N. (2006) Crime in the community. A paper given by Nicholas Cowdery, Director of Public Prosecutions, New South Wales, at the New South Wales Teachers Federation Annual Conference, Sydney. http://www.philippedoylegray.com/content/view/45/27/ (accessed 4 December 2009).

Fang, Z. and Schleppegrell, M. (2008) *Reading in the Secondary Content Areas: A Language-based Pedagogy*. Ann Arbor: University of Michigan Pres.

Gee, J. (2003) *What Computer Games Have to Teach us about Learning and Literacy*. New York: Palgrave Macmillan.

Hertzberg, M., Foord, K. and Manga, M. (2006) Dramatically 'e'ngaged. In Fair Go Team, *School is for me: Pathways to Student Engagement*. Sydney: Priority Schools Funding Program, NSW Department of Education and Training, 25-32.

Lewis P. (2007) *How we Think but not in School: A Storied Approach to Teaching*. Rotterdam: Sense Publishers.

New South Wales Legislative Council (2001) *Select Committee on the Increase in Prisoner Population, Final Report*. New South Wales Parliament.

Qualifications and Curriculum Authority (2009) *Assessing Pupils' Progress: Assessment at the Heart of Learning*. http://curriculum.qcda.gov.uk/key-stages-3-and-4/assessment/Assessing-pupils-progress/index.aspx (accessed 2 December 2009)

Rosen M. (2005) Children's reading. In C.Powling (ed.) *Waiting for a Jamie Oliver: Beyond Bog-Standard Literacy*. Reading: National Centre for Language and Literacy.

Simpson, A. (2008) *Reading under the Covers: Helping Children to Choose Books*. Marrickville: Primary English Teaching Association.

Unsworth, L., Thomas, A. and Bush, R. (2004) The role of images and image text relations in group 'basic skills tests' of literacy for children in the primary years. *Australian Journal of Language and Literacy* 27 (1): 46-65.

van Leeuwen, T. (2000) It was just like magic – a multimodal analysis of children's writing. *Linguistics and Education* 10: 273-305.

Notes

[1] **Frances Christie** is Honorary Professor of Education and of Linguistics at the University of Sydney and Emeritus Professor of Language and Literacy at the University of Melbourne. She has worked for many years in language and literacy education and has had a considerable research and publishing record in the area. Recent books have included: *Classroom Discourse Analysis: A Functional Perspective* (London and New York: Continuum, 2002); *Language Education in the Primary Years* (Sydney: University of NSW Press, 2005); with J.R. Martin (eds.), *Language, Knowledge and Pedagogy: Functional Linguistic and Socio-*

logical Perspectives (London and New York: Continuum, 2007); with B. Derewianka, *School Discourse: Learning to Write across the Years of Schooling* (London and New York: Continuum, 2008).

Alyson Simpson is a senior lecturer at the Faculty of Education and Social Work at the University of Sydney. She teaches in undergraduate and postgraduate pre-service teacher programmes and supervises research candidates studying in the area of literacy/English education. Her research projects have examined designs for e-learning and concepts of visual literacy in higher education and primary schools. She is the co-author of *Children's Literature and Computer Based Teaching* (London: Oxford University Press, 2005) and author of *Reading under the Covers: Helping Children to Choose Books* (Newtown: Primary English Teaching Association, 2008).

Index

Aboriginal children 5, 88
abuse *see* Youth Off The Streets
action learning 66
adolescents 15, 46
    and literacy 5, 10, 15, 16-20; *see also* Youth Off The Streets
American National Institute for Early Education Research 76
Arts, the 5-6, 56-67
    definitions of 56-58
    importance of 58
    and learning 58-61
    teaching of 57
assimilation 117
asylum seekers 117
attachment theory 89
Attention Deficit Hyperactivity Disorder (ADHD) 90
Australian Department of Immigration and Citizenship (DIAC) 114
Australian Language and Literacy Policy 1-2
Australian Social Inclusion Board 84
autism spectrum disorder 90

'back-to-basics' reading programmes 2
behavioural change 90, 91
benchmarking 63
books and children's lack of exposure to 73
Breakthrough to Literacy Programme 12

Cambourne's conditions of learning 91-92
Center for Educational Research and Innovation, OECD 43-44
children with disabilities 95
Children's Information Service, UK 82
Circle of Courage 87-88
classroom interaction 102-103
collaborative group learning 35, 36, 37, 59
'common' schools 11
confidence, lack of in children 73
congruent grammar 18
community service 93-96
cultural bereavement 121

decontextualised words 74
Department of Community Services, NSW 77, 96
Department of Education and Training, NSW 120
Department of Juvenile Justice, NSW 96
Department of Education and Training, NSW, Ethnic Affairs Priorities Statement 120, 122
differences between speech and writing 6, 18, 19
digital and mobile technology 24
    and literacy 25-37
drama 59, 61-62, 67
drug dependency *see* Youth Off The Streets
dysfunctional communication 102

early childhood intervention 1, 4, 74-77, 131
    in Australia 83, 84
    in Sweden 81, 82, 84

in the UK 81-82, 84
early reading 50-51, 107
Early Years Development and
    Childcare Partnerships, UK 81-
    82
Early Years Learning Framework,
    Australia 83
EDEN project *see* Education
    Development Empowerment
    Now
educational reform 11
    as means for breaking cycle of
    abuse and poverty 88, 98, 102
Education Development
    Empowerment Now (EDEN)
    project 5, 93-96, 134
elementary education 10-12
employment and literacy 5
energy, lack of in disadvantaged
    children 73
English in the National Curriculum,
    UK 2
ESL 102, 103, 120
excursions, importance of 72

generalisation and judgement in
    writing 16, 19
genre-based approach to writing 103
giftedness 90
grammar 14

High Scope Perry Preschool Study 76
Home Interaction Program, Australia
    83
home reading 103-105, 107, 108
'homelands movement' 101
homelessness *see* Youth Off The
    Streets
hot-seating 61, 62, 64, 65
Howard Liberal government 118

illiteracy 12
imagination 56, 57, 58
    and literacy 133-34

imaginative writing 59
    and teaching 62-66, 67
inclusiveness 90
Indigenous education *see* Aboriginal
    children; Pitjantjatjara
Individual Learning Plan (ILP) 97
inequality *see* social disadvantage;
    social justice
informal influences on learning 79
Information and Communication
    Technologies (ICT) 4, 26, 32,
    44, 45
integration of pre-school and
    kindergarten 79
International Adult Literacy Surveys 3
International Literacy Year, 1990 12-
    13
Internet 26, 37

journal writing 110-11

Key College, Macquarie Fields
    Campus *see* Education
    Development Empowerment
    Now (EDEN) project

language
    changes from childhood to
    adolescence 16, 47-52
    development 13
    enrichment 97
    lack of in socially disadvantaged
    children 71-73
    and patterns 107
    theory of 9, 10
Learning by Design 26-27
learning difficulties 90
'learning to learn' strategies 97
learning from reading 105
letter–sound correspondence 60, 110
Literacy for All: The Challenge for
    Australian Schools 2
literacy
    and the Arts 5-6, 56-67

benefits of 4, 7
community interest in 1
and construction of meanings 3
critical literacy 52, 60, 63
cultural literacy 122
definitions of 2, 9-10, 12-13, 24
and design 31-32
dichotomies in literacy
education 9, 10
digital literacy 24, 25, 28, 30,
31-32, 36
as discrete skills 9, 11, 13, 15
early intervention teaching of
literacy 1, 4, 74-77, 131
education in the nineteenth
century 10, 11, 12
education in the twentieth
century 46
education in the twenty-first
century 25
emancipatory literacy 2, 3
emergent literacy 74
history of the word 'literacy' 6,
9, 12-13, 24, 132
and Information and
Communication Technologies
(ICT) 4, 26, 32, 44, 45
and learning of knowledge 6
measurement of 2
multiliteracies 6, 25, 26-27, 28,
30, 34, 35, 36, 122, 132-33
multimodality 24, 26, 30, 52,
132-33
new literacies 6, 25-26, 27-28
and oppression 2, 3
and portable knowledge 52
and primary education 28-32,
41, 46-52, 132
print-based 24, 28, 30, 34, 35, 36
reasons for teaching 130
and refugee children 116, 120,
121-23
scientific 33
and self-worth 5, 60

school literacy 46-52, 74
and secondary education 5, 41,
46-52, 105-106, 131, 132
significance accorded to in
national development 2
as single global skill 12, 59
and social disadvantage 5, 75
and social justice 4, 73, 74
and social responsibility 4, 40-
53, 134
as sociocultural phenomenon 3,
71-84, 122
as taught in colonising language
2
and teacher education 1
and technology 26-37
testing 51-52, 60, 133
theories 27
wars 107
see also reading, writing
literature
authentic 57, 62, 63, 67
contrived reading materials 60
picture books 57
Lizard Project, the 93-96

mandatory detention 118, 125-26
monitorial systems 10
multiculturalism 117, 120
multiliteracies 6, 25, 26-27, 28, 30,
34, 35, 36, 122, 132-33
multimodality 24, 26, 30, 52, 132-33
mutism, selective 73

National Commission on Writing 15
National Curriculum, Australia 25
*National Declaration on Educational
Goals for Young Australians* 44
National English Curriculum,
Australia 2
National Inquiry into Literacy,
Australia 2, 13-14
National Literacy Strategy, UK 15-16
National Quality Standards for Child

Care and Preschool, Australia 83
new literacies 6, 25-26, 27-28
New London Group 26
New South Wales K–6 science
    syllabus 32
No Child Left Behind (NCLB), USA
    1
Nuffield/Schools Council Programme
    in Linguistics and English
    Teaching 12

OECD 3, 43-44, 81, 82
OFSTED 82
Old Deluder Satan Law 42, 45

parent–child reading 103-105, 107,
    108
pedagogy 3, 6, 109
petrol sniffing 101, 102
phonemic awareness 107
phonics 14, 107, 110
Pitjantjatjara 101-104, 107
play 57, 58, 77
positive relationships 92, 108
poverty and disadvantage 71-84
process drama 59, 61-62, 67
pre-service teacher education 1
Primary Connect 79
primary education and literacy 28-32,
    41, 46-52, 132
Programme for International Student
    Assessment (PISA) 14, 15
Public Instruction Act, NSW 11
punishment 91, 92-93

racism 117, 120
RAND Corporation 75
rapport 89, 96, 97
readers' theatre 61, 64
readiness for learning 75, 76, 78-80,
    105
reading 6, 13-16
    Detailed Reading 111, 112
    importance for enjoyment and

critical thinking 133
    learning from 105
    teaching of 10, 11, 20, 108, 109
reading and writing 6, 12, 42
    as discrete skills 11, 20, 106
*Reading First Impact Study: Final
    Study*, USA 25
reading for meaningful
    communication 14
reading strategies 30, 103,104
Reading to Learn Programme 109-13
refugee children and youth 5, 118-26,
    134
    best policy in enhancing literacy
        among 126
    educational needs of 116, 120,
        121-23
    and experience of mandatory
        detention 125-26
    health and welfare needs of 120-
        21
    legal status of 118-19
    needs of those lacking formal
        education 123-24
    and new gender roles 124
    and self-esteem 124
    statistical invisibility of 119-20
    unaccompanied 124-25
refugee settlement in Australia 5, 117-
    18
rehabilitation 87
respect 98, 99
responsibility 92, 98
restorative justice 92
rights of the child 73, 77
Rose Report on the Primary
    Curriculum, UK 1, 5, 6, 14, 24

scaffolding learning 6
Scaffolding Reading and Writing for
    Indigenous Children in School 6,
    103, 104
'school to prison pipeline' 5, 74, 75,
    131

school readiness gap 76, 79
    narrowing the gap 77-78
schooling
    in ancient Athens 41-42, 45, 58
    in early Puritan communities in USA 42, 45
    importance of a welcoming school 121-23
    and social responsibility 41-43, 46, 47
secondary education and literacy 5, 41, 46-52, 105-106, 131, 132
Service Learning projects 93, 96
'skilled migration' 118
social contexts of texts for reading 108
social disadvantage 5, 71-74, 75, 76, 79, 88, 119,
    and educational outcomes 106
    inter-generational nature of 83
social inclusiveness 84
social justice 4, 73, 74, 84, 113, 119, 130, 134
social networking 31, 34, 36
social skills acquisition 78
social responsibility 40-41
    and the future 43-46
    and schooling 41-43, 53, 67, 84
social welfare agencies and schools 4, 72, 80, 84, 134
speech impediments 73, 80
speech therapy 80, 84
'Starting Strong' 81
state-sponsored compulsory education 10, 20
storytelling 58, 60, 61-62
strength-based programmes 90, 126
stress and anxiety 73, 90
Sunday schools 10

supportive social policy 81-83
Sure Start, UK 82

Tampa Incident 117
Technical and Further Education (TAFE) 96
technical language 19, 33
tertiary education and literacy 32-36
text analysis 111

unemployment and low literacy 3
UNESCO 12
United Nations High Commission for Refugees (UNHCR) 116
United Nations Convention on the Rights of the Child 117
Uniting Care Burnside 81

Volksschule 11

Web 2.0 interactions 34, 37
White Australia Policy 117
Whitlam Labor government 117
whole-language methods 107
World Bank Report on Reshaping Economic Geography 3
writing 6, 9, 11-12, 15, 31, 108
    developmental phases in 16, 19-20
    Joint Rewriting 111, 112
    learning to write 110
written language and speech 6, 18, 19

youth displacement 77-88
Youth Off The Streets 5, 87-99, 130, 134
    assumptions behind 89-93
    entry to programme 96-98

CPSIA information can be obtained
at www.ICGtesting.com
Printed in the USA
BVOW06s0347060118

504439BV00002B/2/P